Uneasy Citizenship

Uneasy Citizenship

Embracing the Tension in Faith and Politics

DANIEL BENNETT

CASCADE *Books* · Eugene, Oregon

UNEASY CITIZENSHIP
Embracing the Tension in Faith and Politics

Copyright © 2024 Daniel Bennett. All rights reserved. Except for brief quotations in critical publications or reviews, no part of this book may be reproduced in any manner without prior written permission from the publisher. Write: Permissions, Wipf and Stock Publishers, 199 W. 8th Ave., Suite 3, Eugene, OR 97401.

Cascade Books
An Imprint of Wipf and Stock Publishers
199 W. 8th Ave., Suite 3
Eugene, OR 97401

www.wipfandstock.com

PAPERBACK ISBN: 978-1-6667-0231-6
HARDCOVER ISBN: 978-1-6667-0232-3
EBOOK ISBN: 978-1-6667-0233-0

Cataloguing-in-Publication data:

Names: Bennett, Daniel, author.

Title: Uneasy citizenship : embracing the tension in faith and politics / Daniel Bennett.

Description: Eugene, OR: Cascade Books, 2024 | Includes bibliographical references and index.

Identifiers: ISBN 978-1-6667-0231-6 (paperback) | ISBN 978-1-6667-0232-3 (hardcover) | ISBN 978-1-6667-0233-0 (ebook)

Subjects: LCSH: Christianity and politics. | Church and social problems—United States. | United States—Social problems.

Classification: HN37.A6 B5 2024 (paperback) | HN37 (ebook)

05/09/24

For Henry, Margaret, and James

Contents

Acknowledgments		ix
Introduction		xi
1	How We Got Here	1
2	The Polarization Problem	18
3	The Culture Shift	34
4	A Better Political Engagement	52
5	Liberalism, Pluralism, and Christian Politics	75
6	Investing in Institutions	95
7	Comfort in the Uncomfortable	116
Bibliography		129
Index		145

Acknowledgments

Mere Orthodoxy's Jake Meador once wrote, "One of the persistent problems right now in evangelical media and publishing is that we have historians and sociologists trying to do theological or biblical work and unless you are *extremely* good, you probably can't pull that combo off."[1] This struck a chord with me for two reasons: First, because it's true; and second, because I saw myself in the criticism. I am not a sociologist, but I am a social scientist. And while I do not consider this book a work of theology, it is meant to be one of discipleship. I can only hope the pages that follow have met this high burden. I'll let you, dear reader, be the judge.

In writing this book I am grateful for the assistance, kindness, and encouragement of many people, probably too many to name. I am thankful for the intellectual and material support from my colleagues and community at John Brown University, especially Aminta Arrington, Ed Ericson, and Trisha Posey. I am thankful for the able research assistance of Caleb Hall, Natalie Rogers, and Sarah Grace Smith, who read and critiqued chapter drafts and found information when I needed it. And I am thankful for my students for prompting me to think about the implications of faithful political engagement on equipping the next generation of Christian leaders. Working with such great students on a daily basis is both rewarding and humbling.

I am thankful for the leadership at the Initiative on Faith and Public Life at the American Enterprise Institute—especially Mitchell Baron, Tyler Castle, Aryana Petrosky, and Jeff Pickering—for putting together such enriching faculty workshops, including those that prompted this book. I am thankful to institutions like the Acton Institute and Hillsdale College for organizing thoughtful events for faculty from across the spectrum of

---

1. Meador, "One of the Persistent Problems."

Acknowledgments

American conservatism. And I am thankful for the Center for Christianity and Public Life for assembling such an impressive network of Public Life Fellows, and for allowing me to contribute to their important work.

I am thankful for being able to work with such interesting people outside of my university, including the American Values Coalition and Neighborly Faith—these groups embody a rooted and passionate commitment to pluralism, for which I am grateful. I am thankful for occasional conversations with Dave Carroll, Carmen Laberge, Deverin Muff, and Amar Peterman, each of whom helped me develop and sharpen the arguments in this book in one way or another. I am also thankful for the faculty and staff at Union University for inviting me to their campus to talk about these things with their excellent students.

I am thankful for the editorial support from everybody at Cascade Books for helping to shepherd this book through the production process. I am also thankful for Kim Colby, Barry Corey, Shirley Hoogstra, Michael Lindsay, Russell Moore, Kim Phipps, and Chip Pollard for speaking with me about the challenges and opportunities for Christian higher education and institutions in the years ahead.

Most importantly, I am thankful for the support and love from my friends and family. For Brad Edwards, Matt Emmons, Jarrod Heathcote, and the entire "Porch Night" group—thank you for such great conversations and for striking the perfect balance between the sacred and the profane. For Nick Cornett, Nathan McKinney, Kevin Sonoff, Justin Sweeney, and Win Tse—thank you for your friendship over the years. For my mother, Terri—thank you for your unending interest in my work and well-being, and for your ceaseless love and encouragement. For my wife, Caitlyn—thank you for marrying me, for loving me, and for knowing me better than I know myself. And for my children, Henry, Margaret, and James—thank you for making me a father, by far the best thing that has ever happened to me. This book is for you.

Finally, I listened to a lot of music while writing this book, but I found myself routinely returning to the following: Death Cab for Cutie, Nathan Drake, Incubus, Ennio Morricone, Andrew Peterson, Trent Reznor and Atticus Ross, Tame Impala, and The War on Drugs. It's possible that a particularly inspired turn of phrase or piece of prose is owed to one of these artists.

Introduction

"Jesus said to them, 'Render to Caesar the things that are Caesar's, and to God the things that are God's.' And they marveled at him."[1]

Pastor David Platt had a decision to make.

Platt was in the middle of leading McLean Bible Church's afternoon service. Following his sermon and before he led the congregation in the Lord's Supper, the pastor received word that Donald Trump, the president of the United States, would be making an appearance at the church seeking prayer.

It was Sunday, June 2, 2019. Evangelist Franklin Graham had declared it to be a day of prayer for President Trump and his administration. Graham had become no stranger to encouraging Christians to pray for the president. But this day of prayer had an unmistakable partisan tint to it. In addition to calling people to pray for Trump's wisdom and safety, Graham also said, "President Trump's enemies continue to try everything to destroy him, his family, and the presidency. In the history of our country, no president has been attacked as he has."[2] Graham was essentially telling Christians that praying for Donald Trump necessarily means praying that his political opponents would fail and, by extension, that his agenda would succeed.

Platt would have been aware of this dynamic when he heard of Trump's impending visit. Platt later said he recalled Paul exhorting believers to pray "for all people, for kings and all who are in high positions," in 1 Timothy 2. Platt, therefore, decided to pray for the president. Platt and another pastor met with President Trump offstage for a few moments after he arrived.

---

1. Mark 12:17.
2. Gstalter, "Franklin Graham Calls for 'Special Day of Prayer.'"

Introduction

They reportedly had a chance to share the gospel with him. And then Platt took the stage with Trump and offered the following prayer:

> O God, we praise you as the one universal king over all. You are our leader and our Lord and we worship you. There is one God and one Savior—and it's you, and your name is Jesus. And we exalt you, Jesus. We know we need your mercy. We need your grace. We need your help. We need your wisdom in our country. And so we stand right now on behalf of our president, and we pray for your grace and your mercy and your wisdom upon him.
>
> God, we pray that he would know how much you love him—so much that you sent Jesus to die for his sins, our sins—so we pray that he would look to you. That he would trust in you, that he would lean on you. That he would govern and make decisions in ways that are good for justice, and good for righteousness, and good for equity, every good path.
>
> Lord we pray, we pray, that you would give him all the grace he needs to govern in ways that we just saw in 1 Timothy 2 that lead to peaceful and quiet lives, godly and dignified in every way. God we pray for your blessing in that way upon his family. We pray that you would give them strength. We pray that you would give them clarity. Wisdom, wisdom, the fear of the Lord is the beginning of wisdom. Fools despise wisdom and instruction.
>
> Please, O God, give him wisdom and help him to lead our country alongside other leaders. We pray today for leaders in Congress. We pray for leaders in courts. We pray for leaders in national and state levels. Please, O God, help us to look to you, help us to trust in your Word, help us to seek your wisdom, and live in ways that reflect your love and your grace, your righteousness and your justice. We pray for your blessings on our president toward that end.
>
> In Jesus's name we pray. Amen.[3]

News of this event spread quickly. *The Gospel Coalition*'s Joe Carter lauded Platt for his prayer, writing, "Platt made it clear that our earthly leaders will benefit most when they follow 'the one universal king over all'—King Jesus."[4] On the other hand, Jonathan Merritt claimed Platt "made a bad decision that confused and caused pain among many minorities and

---

3. Foust, "Trump Surprises Evangelical Church with Visit."
4. Carter, "David Platt Prays for President Trump."

Introduction

marginalized Christians."[5] And others were critical of Donald Trump's decision to visit the church in the first place—while acknowledging that it isn't unusual for presidents to visit churches, the Center for Christianity and Public Life's Michael Wear said this unannounced visit was "the co-option of worship, the crashing of a service by the apparatus of the presidency."[6] Something seemingly as simple as praying for an elected official was clearly divisive to believers.

Most of us will never have to make a choice like the one David Platt made that Sunday. That is, the president will likely never show up at our church with the expectation that we will pray for them before an audience of hundreds of fellow believers. At the same time, as Christians we should pray for our leaders as they guide our nation, regardless of how we feel about them and their policies. Just as we should pray for our friends and enemies alike, we do not get to choose which political figures are worthy of our prayers. It is easy to pray for presidents and other elected officials with whom we agree on the major issues of the day. It is harder to pray for those with whom we have profound disagreements, let alone in a way that genuinely lifts them up.

Less than eighteen months later Trump lost the 2020 presidential election to Joe Biden, making Trump the first incumbent president to lose his bid for reelection in a generation. On election night Trump appeared to lead in several key states, but because several states barred counting a record number of absentee and mail ballots until after counting Election Day ballots, over time Biden's lead became clear. When the dust finally settled, Joe Biden had won the same number of electoral votes that Trump won in 2016, along with the largest vote share of any candidate since Barack Obama in 2008. This was not a particularly surprising result. After all, polling had shown Biden with a steady lead—both nationally and in key swing states—for months leading up to Election Day, and the public was largely dissatisfied with Trump's response to a once-in-a-lifetime health crisis and its related economic consequences.

For Eric Metaxas, though, this result was not acceptable. While Trump predictably rejected the outcome as evidence of a concerted, fraudulent conspiracy, Metaxas, generally regarded as a public intellectual among Christian conservatives for his biographies of Martin Luther and Dietrich Bonhoeffer, echoed the president's claims and infused them with religious language.

5. Merritt, "I Believe David Platt Is a Well-Meaning Pastor."
6. Wear, "Presidents Visit Churches—but Not the Way Trump Did."

xiii

Introduction

"Trump will be inaugurated," Metaxas wrote. "For the high crimes of trying to throw a U.S. presidential election, many will go to jail.... And Lincoln's prophetic words of 'a new birth of freedom' will be fulfilled. Pray."[7] Metaxas later cited Jesus's words from Luke 8 while tweeting about supposed evidence of fraud, declaring, "For nothing is secret that will not be revealed, nor anything hidden that will not be known and come to light."[8] And according to Bob Smietana, editor-in-chief at Religion News Service, Metaxas told listeners on a prayer call for Trump's legal efforts to trust in God's sovereignty over the process. "He described the controversy over the election as a walk of faith," Smietana wrote, "one in which Jesus will prevail—and [Metaxas's] nemeses in the church and the media would not."[9]

Of course, none of this came to pass. Donald Trump was not inaugurated for a second term as president, despite unprecedented violence at the US Capitol as Congress was certifying the election for Biden. Still, Metaxas did not shift in his rhetoric, suggesting Biden was a fraudulent and fictional president. "Who is running the country???" Metaxas asked in April. "We know it cannot be Joe Biden, because we watch his 'appearances' and see he is a doddering husk of his former self."[10] And in responding to somebody who accused Biden of stoking racial tensions, Metaxas said, "If the American people actually had elected Joe Biden to the presidency, this would trouble me more."[11]

The first major piece of legislation of the Biden administration was a pandemic relief bill, providing direct payments to Americans, an expanded child tax credit, and much more. But the bill caught the attention of the pro-life Americans for what it didn't include—namely, language prohibiting spending taxpayer money on abortions. Known as the Hyde Amendment (after the original sponsor of the amendment, Rep. Henry Hyde), the language had been standard practice in spending bills for over four decades. In signing the American Rescue Plan into law in March 2021, Biden assured that federal spending could directly support abortions for the first time since 1976.

One group especially aggrieved at this process was Pro-Life Evangelicals for Biden, a coalition of Christian leaders who endorsed Biden's

---

7. Gerson, "Prominent Evangelicals Are Directing Trump's Sinking Ship."
8. Metaxas, "'For Nothing Is Secret That Will Not Be Revealed.'"
9. Smietana, "How Eric Metaxas Went from Trump Despiser to True Believer."
10. Metaxas, "Who Is Running the Country???"
11. Metaxas, "If the American People Actually Had Elected Joe Biden."

INTRODUCTION

candidacy against Donald Trump. In a statement released following the bill's passage, the group said it had expected a conversation with the Biden administration on the issue of abortion. "We publicly supported President Biden's candidacy with the understanding that there would be engagement with us on the issue of abortion and particularly the Hyde Amendment," the group said. "The Biden team wanted to talk to us during the campaign to gain our support, and we gave it on the condition there would be active dialogue and common ground solutions on the issue of abortion. There has been no dialogue since the campaign."[12] One of the group's founders, Richard Mouw, said the decision to remove the Hyde Amendment raised the question of whether pro-life Americans—many of them Christians—are in any way welcome in the Democratic Party.

David Platt's prayer for Donald Trump, the post-election rhetoric of Eric Metaxas, and Pro-Life Evangelicals for Biden's disappointment with the Biden administration illustrate the tension and conflict at the intersection of faith and politics. It is a tired refrain that religion and politics are two topics one should not bring to the dinner table. But for Christians, wrestling with this relationship is unavoidable. We cannot ignore the fact that we live in a fallen world, but we cannot pretend that we are alive for any other reason than to be a witness to a world in dire need of the grace of God through Jesus Christ. And considering what is ultimately at stake, how we go about this matters immensely.

I am a political scientist. I research the intersection of politics, law, and religion in the United States. I am also a college professor. In my teaching, I encourage students to think critically, to write carefully, and to wrestle with some of the most important questions of our (or any) time. But most importantly, I am a Christian. I believe God calls his people to engage the world for his kingdom in every aspect—paraphrasing Dutch theologian and politician Abraham Kuyper, every square inch—of what we do. And yes, this includes politics.

In our current moment, politics is sometimes a dirty word. This is almost certainly true for many Christians, who read the Bible and find it difficult to reconcile the words of Jesus with the political spectacle of our present era. This is definitely true among some of the students I teach. But politics is more fundamental, more essential to our nature than cable news portrays it to be. At its root, politics is not about the self-interest and naked ambition portrayed in the media, the sort of politics that so often turns

---

12. Robertson, "Pro-Life Evangelicals for Biden Feel Betrayed."

people off to the political process. Nor is it solely about power and the allocation of resources in a competitive, scarce environment. Instead, at its most basic level, politics is the interactions we have with one another in shared community. Politics is how we order ourselves. And for Christians, politics is just another opportunity to love our neighbors.

Of course, this is much easier said than done. It is difficult to determine how to use politics and its institutions to love our neighbor, especially when there appears to be more than one "Christian" answer to complex problems. But this difficulty is not an invitation to disengage or disconnect. Instead, it reminds us of the inherent complexity we face as citizens of two kingdoms. Christians live in the difficult position of having to reconcile our identities on earth and in heaven. This balancing act entails juggling political decision-making with foundational, sincerely held commitments. This can be hard. It can be uncomfortable. In fact, given the stakes, it should be.

This is the essence of uneasy citizenship.

WHAT TO EXPECT FROM THIS BOOK

Let me begin by stating what this book is not. It is not a treatise explaining which political positions Christians should hold. While some issues are more likely to unify believers, most leave room for disagreement, even after prayerful reflection and consideration. Nor is it a book calling out certain kinds of political activity by Christians, or lamenting the marriage of certain elements of American Christianity with its two major political parties. Though Christians *should* be cautious about becoming too enamored with partisan politics, this is not inherently bad. Nor is it a book identifying scriptural support and references for different areas of policy and politics in contemporary America. As with anything else, the Bible can tell us a great deal about how we should approach and understand modern political issues. But that is not my purpose here.

Instead, this is a book that looks to reorient the conversation around faith and politics in a time of deep political and cultural divisions. At the risk of sounding alarmist, there is a lot of evidence that our political system is sick. Now, I don't mean that our political institutions are at risk of failing—our constitutional structure is remarkably resilient, despite the hyperbole you may find on social media. But our *system*, with an emphasis on deliberative and engaged citizens? This is, I believe, quite troubled. And

Introduction

faithful citizens should do what we can to understand this, for the purpose of more effectively engaging politics and culture.

Uneasy Citizenship is organized around specific challenges to (and opportunities for) American Christians, as well as a charge to embrace the uneasy citizenship specific to every believer. This means leaning into the tension that sometimes turns Christians off to politics, but it also means not treating politics as the ultimate exercise of our identities. We *should* feel a sense of urgency about engaging politics for the sake of the kingdom, protecting the most vulnerable in our society and using our gifts to serve our communities. But people of faith must not become so enamored with and invested in politics—specifically partisan politics—that it motivates our every action. Put simply, Christians should embrace this tension while refusing to idolize it.

In the first three chapters, I introduce several challenges facing believers as we attempt to engage politics in a manner befitting our identity in Christ. Chapter 1 traces the history of Christian political engagement in the United States, with an eye toward different periods of engagement and how we ended up where we are today. With that history in mind, chapter 2 turns to a problem endemic to American politics: social and political polarization. It is not that we disagree with one another (this, by itself, is not concerning), but we are engaging with and attempting to understand one another less and less. Closing this section, chapter 4 points to future challenges situated at the intersection of faith and political engagement. Some of these challenges—like the tension between protecting religious freedom and recognizing rights for LGBTQ Americans—are arriving now, while others—like demographic shifts and the decreasing importance of religion in people's lives—are emerging more slowly.

While these challenges are serious and pose real problems for people of faith as we strive to engage politically in the twenty-first century, these challenges also offer special opportunities. Chapter 4 argues for a better kind of political engagement for Christians, one that remembers our fellow citizens are made in God's image, emphasizing humility and consistency, and rooting one's identity in Christ instead of in politics. Chapter 5 makes the case for pluralism and *liberalism*—not the political ideology, but the framework guiding Western society for centuries. Specifically, I argue that despite the challenges pluralism and liberalism may present to Christians today, they are still preferable to the alternatives. At the same time, chapter 6 urges Christians to invest in and strengthen faith-based communities—including churches and institutions of higher education—so that we are best prepared to deal with the challenges laid out in earlier chapters. Lastly, chapter 7 offers encouragement to Christians wrestling with what all this means in our daily lives.

THE WORK AHEAD

The challenges outlined earlier in the book are real and will not go away on their own. It is therefore crucial for Christians to proactively confront these challenges in a way that is both strategically wise and consistent with who we are in Christ. Living uneasily with our citizenship will surely be work, but given the stakes and the opportunities, it is work worth doing.

American Christians make difficult decisions regarding political engagement on a regular basis. These choices may not be as visible as David Platt's decision to pray over President Trump or Eric Metaxas's decision to quote the Bible in supporting unfounded claims of electoral fraud, but their impact may be consequential nonetheless. How should Christians vote in an election with two flawed candidates? On what issues should Christians be most vocal? What position(s) should Christians find disqualifying for a candidate or official to hold? To what extent should Christians demand exemplary private behavior from their public servants?

This book will not provide succinct or clear-cut answers to these questions. This is because in most cases, politics and policy is not a black-and-white conversation—there are myriad shades of gray in most questions about government and policy. But this does not mean that there aren't things all Christians can (and, as I argue here, should) do when weighing how to act faithfully in our political engagement. Indeed, as Christians, we acknowledge that the good life does exist, and that all aspects of who we are should illuminate the hope that lives within us.

This book will encourage believers to seriously reflect on what it means to be a Christian citizen in a fallen world, and what this means for our specific actions. Because while the scope of these actions will undoubtedly vary from person to person, sitting back and doing nothing while the waters of society churn steadily along is, frankly, not an option. We are called to do more. Our approach to politics ought to reflect this.

1

How We Got Here

"Our faith as believers in Christ will inevitably have political implications. Christians will not necessarily agree about those implications."[1]

History will likely remember 2020 as the year of the coronavirus pandemic. But that year's summer months brought some of the most intense and prolonged protests to the United States since the civil rights movement. Prompted by the deaths of George Floyd, Breonna Taylor, and Ahmaud Arbery—three Black Americans killed by white police officers (or, in Arbery's case, vigilantes)—activists across the country spilled into the streets demanding reforms to America's criminal justice and policing systems. And while many of these protests were peaceful and measured, several in major cities turned riotous and violent.

It was in this context that Donald Trump took perhaps the most famous walk of his presidency. After clearing neighboring Lafayette Park of its hundreds of protesters, the president walked from the White House to St. John's Episcopal Church, nicknamed "Church of the Presidents" for its proximity to the White House and for the number of presidents who have attended throughout history. St. John's had been damaged during the protests, by both graffiti and a fire set in the basement.

Upon arriving in front of the boarded-up church, the president stood for a moment before being handed a Bible by an aide. He held it at his side in his left hand before examining it with both hands, proceeding to hold it

---

1. Kidd, "Christian Discernment in Civic Engagement and Politics."

in front of his stomach for several seconds. Then, after seemingly debating how to display it, Trump raised the Bible with his right hand, his thumb gripping the book by the front bottom. He appeared resolved, brow furrowed and eyes narrowed. A reporter asked him, "Is that your Bible?" to which Trump responded, "It's *a* Bible."[2]

For Christians across the political spectrum, the reaction to what was essentially a photo op was swift and polarized. Some praised the president, characterizing Trump's actions as a defiant defense of Christian values during a season of chaos and violence. Ralph Reed, a veteran of Christian conservative political activism, told *The Atlantic*, "His presence sent the twin message that our streets and cities do not belong to rioters and domestic terrorists, and that the ultimate answer to what ails our country can be found in the repentance, redemption, and forgiveness of the Christian faith."[3] And the Christian Broadcasting Network's David Brody said, "I don't know about you but I'll take a president with a Bible in his hand in front of a church over far left violent radicals setting a church on fire any day of the week."[4]

Other Christians were less impressed. Michael Gerson, a former speechwriter for George W. Bush, called the photo op "a truly sacrilegious use of the Bible to bless a brutal stunt."[5] And Michael Wear, a veteran of the Obama White House Office of Faith-Based and Neighborhood Partnerships, lamented, "As someone who worked very hard to try to set a standard for responsible, ethical religious engagement from The White House, it is heartbreaking and infuriating to see a POTUS who has fallen short of every standard and broken every sense of propriety and respect and humility."[6]

Donald Trump holding up a Bible was far from the first instance of Christianity merging with politics. Since the earliest days of the church Christians have wrestled with the proper scope of political engagement consistent with our allegiance to God's kingdom. Paul and Peter give directives to the early church in Rome, urging rightly ordered obedience to governing authorities. Augustine wrestled with these essential questions in the aftermath of the collapse of the Roman Empire. Luther, Calvin, and other Reformers responded to contemporary conflicts between church and state amid ongoing religious wars across the European continent. And the list goes on.

2. Montague, "Holding It Aloft, He Incited a Backlash."
3. Coppins, "Christians Who Loved Trump's Stunt."
4. Brody, "I Don't Know about You."
5. Gerson, "Truly Sacrilegious Use of the Bible to Bless a Brutal Stunt."
6. Wear, "As Someone Who Worked Very Hard."

How We Got Here

Even so, the United States has facilitated a unique relationship between religion (historically, Christianity) and the public square. Its constitutional structure bars the government from interfering in most religious activity while at the same time protecting the free exercise of religion. This has led to a religious culture unmatched in advanced industrial nations, and one in which religious citizens, including Christians, are emboldened to advocate for political outcomes in alignment with their faith traditions. The oft-cited "wall of separation between church and state" does not prohibit advocacy rooted in religion; rather, it limits the government's ability to regulate it.

For Christians, politics is at the very foundation of our uneasy citizenship. Jesus's words in the New Testament imply an active faith, one that inspires both practice and service. "Let your light shine before others," Jesus says, "so that they may see your good works and give glory to your Father who is in heaven."[7] The Christian faith is not a hidden one; it is simultaneously revealed to and confounds the world. In the same way, Christians cannot compartmentalize faith from politics. These concepts are inextricably bound together. Politics, to paraphrase Wear, is an essential venue in which we love our neighbors.

However, in recent decades Christians would be forgiven for expressing exhaustion at the state of our political engagement. Too often, Christians see our brothers and sisters acting in ways inconsistent with the faith, preferring to hold onto power instead of embracing humility or prioritizing political agendas instead of the gospel. The stereotypes are legion: Christians on the left idolize social justice while downplaying the deaths of the unborn and ignoring an increasingly chaotic terrain of gender and sexual identity; Christians on the right worship at the altar of Christian nationalism and ignore the plight of "the least of these"; and those in the middle do not believe firmly in *anything*.

The history of Christian political engagement in the United States is long, complex, and contested. Accounts from theologians, historians, social scientists, and journalists have all painted vivid pictures of what this history looks like, and—crucially—how this history informs political and cultural engagement today. It would be a fool's errand to attempt to answer this question in one book, let alone one book chapter. Instead, in this chapter I will quickly focus on a few of these accounts to highlight the debate over Christian political engagement in the United States—namely, how it started and where it is heading.

---

7. Matthew 5:16.

Admittedly, I am writing about a narrow element of Christian political engagement. Volumes have been written about the Black church's political involvement through American history,[8] as they have about the so-called "religious left" encompassing the mainline Protestant tradition.[9] The history of evangelical political engagement could be told in myriad ways and highlight myriad stories. But in this chapter, I am focusing on the (mostly white) evangelical political tradition.[10] And even then, I am narrowing this discussion to the last hundred or so years.

Why limit the chapter in these ways? For three primary reasons. First, I write as a white evangelical Christian, and this is the story with which I am most familiar and most regularly encounter in my position as a professor at a Christian university and in my membership at a predominantly white church. Second, while I like to think I have a good read on the history of the intersection of American religion and politics, I am decidedly not a historian; these limits are as much for my benefit as for yours. And third, in order to keep the conversation organized and from becoming unwieldy, we simply must have reasonable conditions in place. Put differently, we have to start (and stop) somewhere.

So while this chapter is *a* story of Christian political engagement in American history, it is certainly not *the* story. Still, given the influence of evangelical Christians on American politics over the past several decades, it is an important story. And for evangelical Christians seeking guidance on how to best engage politics and culture in an increasingly messy and disruptive era, it is an essential story.

COMPETING ACCOUNTS OF EVANGELICAL POLITICAL ENGAGEMENT

No history of American Christian political engagement can be exhaustive, even one focused on a specific element of the Christian tradition. Nevertheless, three themes stand out as especially relevant in explaining the emergence of evangelicals engaging in politics in the United States: abortion,

---

8. See, for example, McDaniel, *Politics in the Pews*.

9. See, for example, Jenkins, *American Prophets*.

10. In this chapter I use the terms "evangelical," "conservative evangelical," and "white evangelical" interchangeably. Unless otherwise noted, when you see one of these labels I'm referring to the group of Christians who are generally (though not exclusively) white as well as theologically, culturally, and politically conservative.

strength and power, and race. These themes are not necessarily mutually exclusive, as they may overlap at times and in notable ways. Still, observers might find one more satisfying than others in making sense of evangelical political engagement, especially in the last several decades. In exploring these themes, I want to explain what Christian political engagement has looked like in the past and how it might look in the future. As with any sort of history, the goal is not to simply rehash the past, but to understand the past in order to make sense of the present while preparing for the future.

Abortion

Perhaps the most familiar story for Christians understanding our political engagement is one about abortion—or, more accurately, opposition to abortion. The story goes like this: In 1973 the US Supreme Court issued its decision in *Roe v. Wade*, which effectively legalized abortion across the country.[11] Prior to *Roe*, some states had banned abortion almost entirely, making few exceptions for the procedure beyond the health of the mother. But *Roe* changed this, reading a right to abortion into the already controversial right to privacy, which the court had declared less than ten years earlier.

With *Roe* as established precedent, states could no longer ban abortion altogether. Instead, states were required to treat abortion like a constitutional right. While some restrictions were acceptable (such as prohibitions against late-term elective abortions), others that lacked a defined state interest were seen as violating women's freedoms under the Constitution. This balancing act was further clarified (and complicated) with 1992's *Planned Parenthood v. Casey*, which upheld the *Roe* decision but also stated some restrictions on abortion were permissible so long as they did not impose an "undue burden" on a woman's right to an abortion.[12]

For theologian Francis Schaeffer, *Roe v. Wade* was anathema to the Christian worldview and to the ethic that had defined the American story for generations. Schaeffer's 1981 book *A Christian Manifesto* points to the doctrine of humanism—the notion that mankind is "at the center of all things," thereby focusing the created order not on a sovereign and eternal God, but rather on ourselves—as largely responsible for cultural attitudes toward abortion.[13] In response, Schaeffer called for the very kinds of political

11. *Roe v. Wade*, 410 U.S. 113.
12. *Planned Parenthood of Southeastern Pennsylvania v. Casey*, 505 U.S. 833.
13. Schaeffer, *Christian Manifesto*.

and legal action on abortion that eventually came to dominate American society over the span of two generations; he concluded, "the State must be made to feel the presence of the Christian community."[14]

It is this outrage over the broad legalization of abortion, the argument goes, that triggered the next several decades of evangelical political engagement. Prior to *Roe*, evangelicals had trouble unifying around a specific political issue, even on the issue of abortion. Indeed, in the years leading up to *Roe* more than half of Southern Baptist pastors favored access to abortion in some cases. And in 1971 the Southern Baptist Convention passed a resolution that argued for "a high view of the sanctity of human life" while calling for laws "that will allow for the possibility of abortion under such conditions as rape, incest, clear evidence of fetal deformity, and carefully ascertained evidence of the likelihood of damage to the emotional, mental, and physical health of the mother."[15]

The Supreme Court's decision in *Roe* gave evangelicals—and the elected officials courting this bloc's votes—a clear target, an opponent to rally against. In the 1980 presidential election, two-thirds of white evangelicals ditched one of their own—the born-again southerner Jimmy Carter—in favor of a divorced former actor by the name of Ronald Reagan. Why? A major reason has to do with Jerry Falwell's founding of the Moral Majority in 1979, and Falwell's intentional efforts to "yoke his movement to rightist politicians and . . . shape their stance on major matters," including abortion.[16] Even though this relationship has not always been perfect—according to historian Thomas Kidd, "Reagan appointed few evangelicals in his administration, and he grievously disappointed pro-lifers by appointing Sandra Day O'Connor to the Supreme Court"[17]—the alliance between white evangelicals and Republican politics has nevertheless been strong. Most recently, it culminated with another odd ally of this community (Donald Trump), who pledged to appoint Supreme Court justices who would one day overturn *Roe v. Wade*.[18]

This explanation for evangelical political engagement is compelling for a couple of reasons. First, the rise of modern conservative evangelical political activism pretty clearly followed the Supreme Court's decision in

14. Schaeffer, *Christian Manifesto*, 120.
15. Roach, "How Southern Baptists Became Pro-Life."
16. Haberman, "Religion and Right-Wing Politics."
17. Kidd, *Who Is an Evangelical?*
18. Mangan, "Trump."

Roe. Prior to this, evangelicals were simply not as prevalent or cohesive on the American political scene as they would be in the decades that followed. Evangelical political groups looked very different pre- and post-*Roe*. Yes, organizations like the John Birch Society were founded in the 1950s to oppose communism and support social conservatism, while interest groups like the Eagle Forum were instrumental in opposing the Equal Rights Amendment in the 1970s. But larger entities like the Christian Coalition and Moral Majority took shape in the 1980s alongside the "Reagan Revolution," with smaller yet important groups like the Family Research Council, Concerned Women for America, and the American Family Association also developing during this era. For all of these actors, opposition to abortion was a necessary and unifying force.

Moreover, at an individual level, opposition to abortion became a clarion call for evangelicals in making political decisions. Since 1980, white evangelicals have slowly but steadily become more pro-life in public opinion on abortion.[19] At the same time, evangelicals have become a virtual monolith in presidential elections: since 2004, at least 75 percent of evangelicals supported the GOP candidate for president.[20] This is partly due to these candidates' prioritizing opposition to abortion in their electoral platforms, even when the candidates themselves—especially Reagan and Trump—had checkered histories on abortion as a matter of policy. And though abortion was not the only issue driving social conservatives in the direction of the Republican Party, it was certainly an important one. "After all," writes scholar Bradley Onishi, "what's worse than someone who wants to hurt children?"[21] This, combined with the Democratic Party's increasing embrace of pro-choice policies, all but sealed the deal for many evangelicals.[22]

Andrew Lewis, an expert on American religion and politics, argues in *The Rights Turn in Conservative Christian Politics* that abortion has not just driven evangelical political engagement, but it actually shaped *other* parts of the movement's advocacy. For example, since *Roe*, the predominant

---

19. Lewis, *Rights Turn in Conservative Christian Politics*.
20. Martínez and Smith, "How the Faithful Voted."
21. Onishi, "Is Abortion No Longer Significant for Evangelicals?"
22. In his 1992 campaign for president, Bill Clinton routinely said he believed abortion should be "safe, legal, and rare." By contrast, in his 2020 campaign for president, Joe Biden declared that his administration would work to codify the *Roe v. Wade* precedent into federal law, direct funding to organizations like Planned Parenthood, and remove the so-called Hyde Amendment—which prohibits direct federal funding of abortions—from new legislation.

discourse among conservative, pro-life actors has emphasized the "right to life" when opposing abortion. Lewis argues that adopting rights language in pro-life advocacy eventually led to evangelicals "learning the value of free speech."[23] Lewis explains, "In what began as legal and political support for anti-abortion protestors, evangelicals now leverage free speech arguments to support non-allies and to defeat campaign finance restrictions."[24] For evangelicals, opposition to abortion led to a more complex and sweeping political agenda, including support for First Amendment protections they had previously opposed.[25]

In 2022's *Dobbs v. Jackson Women's Health Organization*,[26] the Supreme Court overturned *Roe v. Wade* and once again allowed states to regulate access to abortion. Andrew Walker of the Southern Baptist Theological Seminary lauded the decision, writing, "The rule of *Roe* is over and its scourge of violence and injustice no more. One of the most important days in American history."[27] And polling after *Dobbs* revealed strong support among white evangelicals for the ruling, with 71 percent saying the court made the right decision in reversing *Roe*.[28] Evangelicals had spent the better part of fifty years coalescing around opposition to abortion. And with the issue again open to democratic deliberation, new questions—such as whether to support increased spending for social programs benefitting women and children, whether to grant legal personhood status to the unborn, and even whether to prosecute mothers who obtain abortions—will likely continue to drive evangelical political engagement in the years ahead.

Strength

If you were a Christian man in the early 2000s, the odds are good that you read John Eldredge's *Wild at Heart*.[29] Eldredge's book was a call for Christian men to recover their untamed and rugged roots, with none other than Jesus held as this standard to which men could aspire. In this way, Jesus was not portrayed as a soft-spoken and gentle leader, the one who claimed

---

23. Lewis, *Rights Turn in Conservative Christian Politics*, 29.
24. Lewis, *Rights Turn in Conservative Christian Politics*, 57.
25. See, for example, Brown, *Trumping Religion*.
26. *Dobbs v. Jackson Women's Health Organization*, 597 U.S. ___.
27. Walker, "Rule of Roe Is over."
28. Pew Research Center, "Majority of Public Disapproves."
29. Eldredge, *Wild at Heart*.

in Matthew 11 that he was "gentle and lowly in heart."[30] Instead, Jesus was passionate, at times angry, and most of all, strong.

This portrayal found a home in many prominent churches of the day, including in Mark Driscoll's Mars Hill Church in Seattle, Washington. Driscoll became known for his passionate and aggressive preaching style, yelling from the pulpit and calling out men in the congregation for not being *real* men. Later it was revealed that Driscoll used an anonymous account to post inflammatory comments on an online message board, where he also said America has become a nation of "sensitive emasculated men."[31]

What, exactly, does this have to do with evangelical political engagement? One answer lies in Kristin Kobes Du Mez's book *Jesus and John Wayne*.[32] Released in 2020 during a contentious presidential election, it tells the story of how many evangelicals came to embrace masculine language and figures in cultural battles, with these values eventually welcomed by certain churches and congregations. Du Mez, a historian at Calvin University, argues that these themes are not relegated to biblical interpretation of spiritual discipleship, matters internal to the church. Instead, she argues, they make sense of how evangelicals have approached politics over the past few decades.

Jesus and John Wayne landed on the *New York Times*' Best Seller list and elicited countless responses from those who grew up in the evangelical environment of the 1980s and 1990s. Some supported Du Mez's portrayal of this movement, saying that it resonated with their experiences. Others were critical of the account, saying it emphasized the wrong things about evangelicalism during this era. Still, the book struck a nerve precisely because of the way in which it told the story of what *really* animated so many evangelical Christians' political beliefs and actions. And that, according to Du Mez, was a desire for power clothed in traditional ideals of masculinity and strength.

According to Du Mez, this kind of strength was exemplified by evangelicals' support for the military and American values during the Cold War. These values expanded into gender roles, too: "The communist threat," Du Mez writes, "positioned women and men in distinct ways; men were to provide for their families and defend the nation, while women were deemed vulnerable and in need of protection. In this way, Cold War masculinity

---

30. Matthew 11:29.
31. Marcotte, "Evangelicals Are Standing Up to Their Own Sexist Leaders."
32. Du Mez, *Jesus and John Wayne*.

was intimately connected to militarism, to the point that they could seem inseparable."[33] Billy Graham—perhaps the most important evangelical of the twentieth century—made these arguments particularly effectively and later advocated for a stronger connection between evangelicals and the halls of power. This approach is clearly seen in Graham's 1969 letter to Richard Nixon, articulating an evangelical rationale for supporting the United States' military efforts in Vietnam.[34]

Du Mez's analysis makes sense of why evangelicals were so quick to turn their backs on Jimmy Carter, who, in many ways, was one of their own—a self-described "born-again" Christian from a southern state. Still, Carter disappointed many evangelicals who had a particular vision of strength they wanted from their leaders. According to Du Mez,

> Carter had overseen what conservatives perceived to be the stunning decline of American strength. On his first day in office he had pardoned draft evaders. He agreed to hand over the Panama Canal and signed a nuclear arms control agreement. He'd allowed the Sandinistas to gain control of Nicaragua and enabled the overthrow of the Shah of Iran. The kidnapping of 52 American hostages at the US embassy in Tehran was an especially humiliating blow.[35]

Carter did not exude the kind of strength evangelicals demanded from those in power. He was, for all intents and purposes, a "wimp."[36]

Compare these evangelicals' dissatisfaction with Jimmy Carter to their support for Lt. Col. Oliver North, a member of President Reagan's National Security Council at the center of the Iran-Contra scandal. Iran-Contra involved the United States covertly selling missiles to Iranian military actors—in violation of an arms embargo—and then transferring the money from these sales to right-wing Contra rebels in Nicaragua. After his testimony before Congress, where he admitted to orchestrating this affair, North was convicted of lying to Congress and sentenced to three years in prison.

All this did little to tarnish North's image in the eyes of many evangelicals. Indeed, many in the Christian Right welcomed North into their good graces. Du Mez writes, "Like North, conservative evangelicals defined the greater good in terms of Christian nationalism. It was this conflation

---

33. Du Mez, *Jesus and John Wayne*, 27.
34. Du Mez, *Jesus and John Wayne*, 50.
35. Du Mez, *Jesus and John Wayne*, 101.
36. Du Mez, *Jesus and John Wayne*, 102.

of God and country that heroic Christian men would advance zealously, and by any means necessary, with their resurgent religious and political power."[37] The Carter-North comparison, according to Du Mez, reveals just what appeals to evangelicals in political engagement—and it isn't "niceness."

The stories at the heart of *Jesus and John Wayne* were so resonant—positively or negatively—because they are so historically prolific. It is, of course, possible to have grown up in an evangelical community and not witnessed firsthand the kinds of obsessions with power and traditional, masculine "strength" Du Mez documents in her book. Nor is it automatically bad for a church to focus on equipping men to be strong to lead their families through an increasingly complicated world. One of the brilliant things about *Christianity Today*'s *The Rise and Fall of Mars Hill* podcast series was its acknowledgment that, despite the failings of church leadership and the potential for abuse in this structure, there were undeniably good things to come from this community—things like previously immature and unserious men becoming committed to their wives and families.[38]

But it is difficult not to see the kinds of fascination with power and strength among evangelicals in today's politics. One reason for this is a reaction, or backlash, to what evangelicals (and conservatives in general) see as more extreme positions taken by those on the left. A refrain during the Trump's 2016 campaign—and eventually, his presidency—was "But he fights!," a belief that while Trump the man is no angel, he at least was willing to push back against an increasingly unhinged series of political opponents. This characterization of Trump as a fighter extends to every aspect of his presidency, including his determination to stand by Supreme Court nominee Brett Kavanaugh after he was accused of sexual assault during an incident in his youth.[39]

Florida's Ron DeSantis has been touted as a potential successor to Trump's brand of politics precisely because of his propensity for aggressive responses to his opponents, albeit in a more strategic and measured way than Trump displayed.[40] "The Florida governor," according to the *New Yorker*, "channels the same rage as the former President, but with greater

---

37. Du Mez, *Jesus and John Wayne*, 117.

38. *Christianity Today*, "Rise and Fall of Mars Hill." In episode 1's "Who Killed Mars Hill?" host Mike Cosper first discusses this dynamic, beginning at around the eleven minute mark.

39. Griswold, "Instead Of Praising Roe's Death, Russell Moore Trashes Trump."

40. Lowry, "Ron DeSantis and the New Republican Party."

discipline."[41] And Ted Cruz, the Texas senator who has touted his "personal relationship with Jesus Christ" as central to his life,[42] exemplified this approach when he introduced himself at a conference in 2022: "My name is Ted Cruz, and my pronoun is 'kiss my ass.'"[43] Anecdotally, these brutish appeals for conservatives—and the evangelicals comprising a large bloc of them—is consistent with the history told in *Jesus and John Wayne*. And though it is an imperfect and incomplete frame, it is undeniably insightful.

Race

To some, it is not opposition to abortion or an emphasis on strength and masculinity that best explains evangelical political engagement. Rather, it is race. Consider the uproar over "critical race theory" (CRT) in churches, seminaries, and other Christian institutions. Drawn from the larger academic field of critical theory—which says that social structures are the primary cause of conflicts among people—CRT maintains that there are institutional explanations for racial conflict in America that have little to do with individual behavior. CRT argues that these conflicts are engrained in the fabric of American society and can only be confronted and addressed with intentional and proactive efforts; simply pursuing "colorblindness," according to CRT, is insufficient.

In a sense, the controversy over CRT is just the latest example of Americans expressing hesitance to discuss the nation's history of racial conflicts and injustices. "CRT" has, for some, become shorthand for any conversation about race and contemporary society. Christopher Rufo, one of the leading drivers of opposition to CRT in recent years, acknowledged as much when speaking to the *New Yorker*:

> We've needed new language for these issues. "Political correctness" is a dated term and, more importantly, doesn't apply anymore. It's not that elites are enforcing a set of manners and cultural limits, they're seeking to reengineer the foundation of human psychology and social institutions through the new politics of race. It's much more invasive than mere "correctness," which is a mechanism of social control, but not the heart of what's happening. The other frames are wrong, too: "cancel culture" is a vacuous term and

---

41. Filkins, "Can Ron DeSantis Displace Donald Trump?"
42. Bailey, "Here's What We Know about the Faith of Sen. Cruz."
43. Slisco, "Ted Cruz Tells Students His Pronoun Is 'Kiss My A**' in Gender Identity Jab."

doesn't translate into a political program; "woke" is a good epithet, but it's too broad, too terminal, too easily brushed aside. "Critical race theory" is the perfect villain.[44]

By framing any conversation about race—in history, in existing social conflicts, or in public policy—through the lens of CRT, it is easier to convince people that these conversations should not be happening at all.[45]

This debate over CRT is far from the first instance of race dividing the church in America. In their book *Divided by Faith*, sociologists Michael Emerson and Christian Smith highlight persistent and deep cleavages within Christian churches on racial lines. They acknowledge that while religion can play an important role in tearing down overtly racist structures and practices—see, for example, the religious foundations of the abolitionist and civil rights movements—it cannot always bridge deeper interpersonal gaps. "Religion in America," they write, "can serve as a moral force in freeing people, but not in bringing them together are equals across racial lines."[46] This has real implications for how Christians do politics.

Historian Randall Balmer is one of the leading proponents of the idea that race best makes sense of evangelicals' political activity over the past several decades. Balmer takes direct aim at the abortion narrative in his book *Bad Faith: Race and the Rise of the Religious Right*, calling the narrative "the Religious Right's most cherished and durable myth."[47] Instead, Balmer argues, evangelical Christians were mostly motivated by the government's efforts to prohibit racial segregation in private education, exemplified by the Internal Revenue Service's actions against Bob Jones University, a private Christian college in South Carolina.

In 1971, a federal judge ruled that the IRS could remove a private school's tax-exempt status if that school was engaged in racial discrimination.[48] After refusing to admit Black students at all, Bob Jones University changed course and began allowing Black students to enroll but stipulated that interracial relationships would be prohibited. The IRS was not satisfied with this arrangement, and in 1976 informed the university that it would be losing its tax-exempt status. Eventually, the Supreme Court ruled in 1983 that the IRS did not violate the First Amendment when it removed Bob

---

44. Wallace-Wells, "How a Conservative Activist Invented the Conflict."
45. McCaulley, "Racial Justice Debate Needs Civil Discourse, Not Straw Men."
46. Emerson and Smith, *Divided by Faith*, 18.
47. Balmer, "Evangelical Abortion Myth."
48. *Green v. Connally*, 330 F. Supp. 1150.

Jones' tax-exempt status, saying the government's interest in preventing racial discrimination outweighed potential constitutional concerns.[49]

Balmer recounted a conversation with one of Bob Jones' administrators, who told him that the episode "alerted the Christian school community about what could happen with government interference."[50] If the government could interfere with the day-to-day operations of Christian schools, the thinking went, other interference would not be far behind. Conservative Christians began to mobilize, Balmer's account goes, and the rest is history.[51] Balmer believes that while abortion eventually moved to the top of the list of evangelical Christians' concerns in politics—spurred by the work of Francis Schaeffer and the activism of interest groups—it was not abortion that kick-started conservative Christians' political engagement. "Although abortion had emerged as a rallying cry by 1980," he continued, "the real roots of the religious right lie not the defense of a fetus but in the defense of racial segregation."[52]

Others have found this race narrative convincing, too. In his book *White Too Long*, social scientist Robert Jones argues that white evangelicals have tended to mesh worldview with biblical interpretation (an inevitable practice, he concedes), to the alienation of our nonwhite brothers and sisters in the church. Jones writes,

> While their fellow Black Christians were reading liberation stories from Exodus and prophets such as Amos and Hosea who were calling for social and economic justice, white evangelicals stayed focused more narrowly on the gospels and the writings of Paul to early Christian churches, which were interpreted more easily to be about salvation, right relationships, maintaining order, and keeping the peace.[53]

---

49. *Bob Jones University v. United States*, 461 U.S. 574.

50. Balmer, "Real Origins of the Religious Right."

51. Attorney Jon Whitehead critiqued this argument in an essay for *The Gospel Coalition*, saying that Balmer had misrepresented a prominent activists' comments about what prompted conservative Christian political engagement in this arena. It wasn't, Whitehead argues, a desire to maintain segregated private schools, but rather opposition to what they saw as mandated affirmative action in exchange for the schools keeping their tax-exempt status. "Most were not defending segregation," Whitehead wrote. "Many were outraged that even churches opposed to discrimination would be lumped in with the segregationists." See Whitehead, "Fact-Checking Randall Balmer's Urban Legend."

52. Balmer, "Real Origins of the Religious Right."

53. Jones, *White Too Long*, 101–2.

This tendency amounts to an infusion of what Jones calls "white supremacy" with Christianity. And given the relationship between race, religion, and political behavior—white evangelicals and Black Protestants, despite nearly identical theological orthodoxy, rarely vote for the same candidates—this has real implications for how evangelicals do politics. Jones concludes his book with optimism, though, writing to his fellow white Christians: "Just as Cain was separated from his natural family, we have allowed white supremacy to separate us not just from our black brothers and sisters but also from a true sense of who we are. . . . [But] there's hope in the Genesis story: Even for the guilty and unrepentant Cain, God acts to preserve the possibility of a new future."[54]

Historian Jemar Tisby is also convinced of the role race has played in evangelical political engagement. After tracing the troubled relationship between white evangelicals and racial concerns throughout American history, Tisby arrives at the emergence of "law-and-order politics" of the Nixon years. This rhetoric is connected to Nixon's "Southern strategy," given its emphasis on appealing to southern white voters dissatisfied with what they saw as an increasingly tumultuous society following the civil rights movement and the political chaos of the 1960s. Importantly, Tisby writes, "Politically conservative elected officials aimed to recruit not only white male voters in the South but white evangelicals as well."[55] These were historically Democratic voters ensconced in Franklin Roosevelt's New Deal coalition, but were increasingly finding themselves out of step with the changing Democratic Party.

As the Southern strategy took shape, the story goes, this new alliance laid the foundation for the Religious Right that helped give rise to Ronald Reagan. Crucially, Tisby says, "The Religious Right's own statement of political objectives . . . demonstrates its troubling compromise with racism by promoting policies that failed to advance or support black civil rights."[56] For example, while conservative Christians vehemently opposed communism, Tisby argues many evangelicals came to equate *any* "liberal" policy—including those aimed at addressing racial issues—as connected to communism. This eventually aligned with the GOP's platform on economics and taxes, favoring tax cuts for corporations and reduced spending on social programs. "Although their intentions may have been varied," Tisby

---

54. Jones, *White Too Long*, 232.
55. Tisby, *Color of Compromise*, 158.
56. Tisby, *Color of Compromise*, 170.

concludes, "in terms of political impact the Religious Right failed to demonstrate a clear commitment to black advancement."[57]

In a 2022 survey from Lifeway Research, about half of Protestant pastors said that racism is more of a problem for the church than CRT, while about 30 percent said CRT was more dangerous than racism.[58] And while some Christian leaders and authors have found CRT useful in explaining the insidious nature of sin, others are concerned that CRT can only divide the body of Christ. In an interview with Fox News, conservative theologian Voddie Baucham said, "Critical race theory is at odds with Christianity because it takes the problem of racism out of the individual heart and puts it out there somewhere in systems and structures."[59] CRT may be a new iteration of conflicts among evangelicals regarding race and politics, but it is hardly the first. And if you find this narrative convincing, it will hardly be the last.

WHERE WE'VE BEEN, WHERE WE ARE, AND WHERE WE'RE GOING

We have no shortage of explanations about what has driven Christian engagement in American politics and culture. In addition to these narratives, Kevin Kruse argues that the best explanation for making sense of contemporary evangelical political engagement is evangelicals' alliance with corporate America against the New Deal of the 1930s.[60] Gerardo Marti argues that the intersection of race and socioeconomic class makes the most sense of evangelical political engagement today.[61] And drawing on the election of Donald Trump, John Fea believes fear is the biggest reason evangelicals behave the way they do in politics.[62] But while these themes have painted a bit of the picture, none of them, on their own, tell the whole story. Each is in some way necessary for understanding evangelical political engagement, but none are sufficient. Read together, they tell us a great deal about where Christians have been in our political engagement, where we are now, and where we are going.

57. Tisby, *Color of Compromise*, 171.
58. Relevant, "Poll."
59. Green, "Critical Race Theory Debate Divides Christians."
60. Kruse, *One Nation Under God*.
61. Marti, *American Blindspot*.
62. Fea, *Believe Me*.

Of these narratives, the one centered on abortion is likely to be most satisfying for conservatives and those sympathetic to the white evangelical community. After all, until its demise in 2022 social conservatives regularly viewed *Roe v. Wade* as among the most odious Supreme Court decisions in American history, alongside the Court's nineteenth-century race decisions in *Dred Scott v. Sandford*[63] and *Plessy v. Ferguson*.[64] The idea of being spurred to political action in the defense of unborn, innocent life is something conservative evangelicals could be proud of, likening these efforts to abolitionists against slavery and civil rights activists. Evangelical political engagement, this narrative goes, is not about control or power but about defending the weakest and most innocent among us.

On the other hand, those with more liberal political views are more likely to find other narratives—such as those stressing strength and racial hierarchy—as more likely and convincing explanations of evangelical political engagement in the twentieth century. Liberal evangelicals are more prone to "punch right" and critique their conservative brethren, emphasizing the need for increased accountability within evangelicalism and looking for ways to improve the church's standing in the eyes of historically marginalized communities. Compared to the narrative on abortion, these narratives portray a more complicated and checkered history of evangelical political engagement, one not devoid of self-interest but rather concerned with maintaining a comfortable status quo.

We cannot be neutral in our reading of these narratives. Our interpretation of the history of evangelical political engagement carries with it unavoidable political implications. Indeed, how we make sense of this history reveals a great deal about how our own ideologies color our vision of the world around us. If we are to truly hold our citizenship uneasily, both tightly and loosely in the service of the kingdom, we must account for the way in which our ideologies are shaping our political engagement. It is to these ideologies—and the political polarization accompanying them—we must next turn.

---

63. *Dred Scott v. Sandford*, 60 U.S. 393.
64. *Plessy v. Ferguson*, 163 U.S. 537.

2

The Polarization Problem

"Americans have rarely been as polarized as they are today."[1]

One of my favorite things to share with students in my introductory American Government and Politics class is the changing complexion of Congress. No, not in terms of the gender of its representatives, or their religion, or their race, but in terms of their *ideology*. In 1952, the House of Representatives was divided amongst Republicans and Democrats, just as it is today. But the ideology of House members looked quite different. On a liberal–moderate–conservative spectrum there were liberal Republicans and conservative Democrats, so that the distribution of House members' ideology resembled a bell curve of sorts, with small tails on either extreme and a larger middle.

Sixty years later, in 2014, the situation changed. That bell curve, with a healthy and robust "middle" section comprised of Republicans and Democrats, had disappeared. In its place was a figure that resembled a bimodal distribution, with almost no overlap in the middle and increasingly high numbers of conservative Republicans and liberal Democrats. Gone were the days of the moderate middle in terms of congressional ideology. Polarization had transformed Congress and its membership, reflecting a steady trend in American society.

As a political scientist, much of my reading, research, and teaching involves polarization, which, in my discipline, refers to people, parties, and

1. Dimock and Wike, "America Is Exceptional in Its Political Divide."

groups growing further apart. This is often discussed in ideological terms, classifying people as either conservative or liberal. But polarization can be found in virtually any aspect of American society, moving beyond the political and influencing what movies and television programs we watch, what sports we enjoy, and even where we eat. More and more, people seem to be looking for ways to highlight their opposition to one another while simultaneously huddling with people who think like them. This is not a recipe for a healthy culture.

As Christians, we are as susceptible to the pitfalls of polarization as our fellow citizens. We live in a fallen world where sanctification does not equal perfectionism. But for Christians tasked with making disciples of all nations and peoples, polarization, while in some sense inevitable, is especially dangerous. Yes, polarization discourages the sort of cooperation and compromise necessary for our system of government. But more importantly, it encourages categorizing people simplistically as either allies or opponents when we should instead be seeing them as made in the image of God.

In this chapter I draw on research from political science to show the pervasive and problematic role polarization plays in American politics and society. I begin in 1950, with a major report from the American Political Science Association on the then-odd state of the Democratic and Republican parties. I then move to a seminal study on the weaknesses in most people's ideologies, written in 1964 but still quite relevant today. Finally, I highlight recent research on polarization, focusing on studies showing how polarization affects people's daily lives, before concluding with the troubling implications of polarization today, ranging from delight in the misfortune of others to support for violence against political opponents.

Polarization of the sort described in this chapter is a significant challenge to Christians' witness to the world. If we are learning to view others with contempt or inherent suspicion as a result of their political inclinations—whether they are fellow Christians or just fellow human beings—we are not giving them the respect they deserve as created in God's image. And when we allow politics to fundamentally alter these relationships, it becomes an idol we must wholeheartedly reject. To combat this challenge, though, we must first understand it.

A SIMPLER TIME FOR POLITICAL PARTIES

The Constitution of the United States does not require political parties for American government, but because of the government's structure, two parties are what we have. *Duverger's law*, named after the French social scientist Maurice Duverger, says that in systems (such as the United States) with "first past the post" elections—where the candidate with the most votes wins regardless of whether they receive a majority—and single-member districts—where only one person represents an area—there will only be two major political parties at any given time. This does not mean that these parties will never change, only that there can only be two seriously competing for power at once. Indeed, this is precisely what we see in the history of American political parties.

The Federalists and Democratic-Republicans dominated the first two decades of national American politics. They included some of the early nation's most influential figures, from Alexander Hamilton and John Marshall to Thomas Jefferson and James Madison. In the decades leading up to the Civil War the Whigs and Democrats rose to prominence, following the fracturing of the Democratic-Republican Party. Republicans and Democrats have been America's predominant political parties since 1854, although the parties have occasionally changed and evolved on significant policy issues. The Democratic Party, for example, enacted Jim Crow laws and vehemently opposed racial integration in the South, yet today supports policies largely in tune with advocates for racial justice.

Despite differences between the parties throughout their history, it was not always easy to determine what made Democrats liberal and Republicans conservative; the parties lacked a constraining ideology. And while the lack of a strong ideology driving American politics may seem like a good thing, it actually poses a problem for governance and elections. When people go to vote, they often use party identification as a heuristic of sorts to aid in their decision-making. Knowing what Republicans and Democrats stand for plays a big role in the process; without it, how is the average American supposed to know which candidate to support? How are voters supposed to hold parties accountable when there isn't a meaningful difference between them?

Observing this problem, in 1950 the American Political Science Association issued a report urging America's two dominant political parties to become more distinct from one another.[2] "For the great majority of Americans," the report stated, "the most valuable opportunity to influence the course of public affairs is the choice they are able to make between the parties in the principal elections." To achieve this goal, the report recommended parties pay closer attention to crafting policy proposals, maintain intraparty unity despite significant regional differences, reform their national nominating conventions, and more.

Reforming America's political parties, the report argued, would yield more predictable and responsible governance due to citizens having greater clarity in what and whom they are voting for. "It is easy to see," the authors said, "that the voter's political choice when confined to candidates without a common bond in terms of program amounts to no more than taking a chance with an individual candidate." If people could not substantively distinguish between their choices in the voting booth, how could they responsibly render judgment on their elected officials? This problem would be rendered moot by a system of stronger, more accountable political parties.

It is quaint to think the largest association of American political scientists once urged Republicans and Democrats to create more distance between them. But these were simpler times. Representing a growing and increasingly diverse population required stronger and more distinct political parties, and eventually, this is what these parties did. Just as crucial to our political system, though, is something largely beyond the parties' control: having informed and politically capable citizens. Are we, though?

HOW IDEOLOGICAL ARE WE?

A little more than a decade after the 1950 APSA report, a young scholar named Philip Converse published what would become one of the most important studies in the history of American political science.[3] And while its title may be opaque to those outside the discipline—"The Nature of Belief Systems in Mass Publics"—its findings are clear and troubling: the average voter is generally not prepared to effectively participate in the American political system.

As a researcher focused on political behavior, Converse's studies focused on how voters made their decisions in the political process. A major element of this decision-making is something called a *belief system*, an

2. "Toward a More Responsible Two-Party System."
3. Converse, "Nature of Belief Systems in Mass Publics (1964)."

overarching scheme structuring and constraining people's beliefs—that is, belief systems hold people's beliefs together in an organized, sensible way.[4] Belief systems are not limited to political beliefs, of course, but this is the domain of most interest to Converse. He asked, to what extent are belief systems responsible for the bulk of people's political preferences?

The answer was surprising, and groundbreaking. Based on information gleaned from American voters in 1956, Converse separated voters into five categories. He concluded that just over 15 percent of the population could be categorized as either "ideologues" or "near-ideologues"—that is, those for whom broad, abstract concepts guided their political decision-making. Making up 45 percent of the population, however, are people who let group interest drive their decision-making. According to Converse,

> These people have a clear image of politics as an arena of group interests and, provided that they have been properly advised on where their groups interests lie, they are relatively likely to follow such advice. Unless an issue directly concerns their group in an obviously rewarding or punishing way, however, they lack the contextual grasp of the system to recognize how they should respond to it without being told by elites who hold their confidence.[5]

This means that nearly half the country is well enough attuned to connect their political positions to their perceived group interest (in this case, via political parties). This is encouraging. On the other hand, when doing so, these same people tend to rely heavily on cues from political elites. This is, as I will explain later, not so encouraging.

The fourth and fifth of Converse's categories highlight a large percentage of Americans who have not given much thought at all to connecting their beliefs to specific policies and political action. He identifies 22 percent of the population as "nature of the times" voters, those who reference particular policies or programs but cannot connect them meaningfully to anything concrete. And Converse concluded about 18 percent of the population's belief systems contained no issue content whatsoever—these are people who expressed loyalty to a political party but could not explain why, nor could they demonstrate any knowledge of what that party stood for.

---

4. Converse defines *belief system* as "a configuration of ideas and attitudes in which the elements are bound together by some form of constraint of functional interdependence" ("Nature of Belief Systems in Mass Publics (1964)," 3).

5. Converse, "Nature of Belief Systems in Mass Publics (1964)," 15.

Converse ultimately concludes it is a problem that belief systems and consistent ideologies do not constrain most Americans' beliefs about public policy. But why? Wouldn't this be a good thing? At first glance, it sure seems like it. After all, doesn't ideology act as blinders on people and make them less likely to compromise and cooperate with those unlike them? Wouldn't our system be better if people were not so dependent on ideology driving their political behavior? As Christians, shouldn't we be encouraged by Converse's results that ideology isn't driving everything around us?

The short answer? No. Converse is certainly not hoping for belief systems to separate people or create division. Still, the fact remains that ideology helps constrain people's belief systems from quickly and easily shifting to suit the temporal needs of elected officials and political elites, and instead be deeply rooted to hold these elites accountable. If people do not have grounded reasons for believing the things they believe when it comes to politics, they are much more likely to be taken advantage of by parties and officials who know they can rely on people's support no matter what they do, so long as they couch their behavior in partisan terms.

Our political system depends on people rewarding (and holding accountable) actors for their performance in office. Without a constrained and cohesive belief system, we are unlikely do this consistently and well. Christians should not seek constrained belief systems to sow division or highlight differences, but rather to promote political stability and accountability in the American system of government.

ARE WE POLARIZED?

Even casual observers of contemporary politics would probably agree that we are a politically polarized people—that is, there are fewer and fewer things that we agree on, and more and more we disagree on. This is certainly the conventional wisdom in American politics these days. But is this true? The answer depends largely on how we define our terms.

Political scientists have been asking questions about polarization for quite some time, and they have tended to do so on two primary levels: at the elite level and the mass level. As to the elite level, there is ample evidence that elites—specifically, elected officials—are polarized and have been getting more polarized for decades. Consider this chapter's earlier reference to how the ideological composition of Congress has changed over time. Using a measure of ideology called NOMINATE scores, political scientists can track how polarized ideology has become over time.[6] And since 1970, congressional ideology has become noticeably more polarized, with greater and greater distance between Left and Right.

But what about the masses? If Converse is right, ideology may not mean all that much for the average American; how, then, can we be polarized? One answer is that polarization may be seen as a trickle-down phenomenon, starting with political elites before making its way to the average voter. If people do not spend much time or energy on their political choices, then they will inevitably vote for one of the options before them. And as these options become further and further apart, so too will the people who must choose between them. The data confirms this: based on responses to the American National Election Study over time, we can see that people have become more and more split on important questions related to the size and scope of government.[7]

Despite this data, there are other perspectives about the prevalence of polarization at the mass level. A lot of this research comes from Stanford University's Morris Fiorina. Fiorina has for years been skeptical of the prevailing narrative concerning polarization in America, preferring a more nuanced understanding of the ways in which the United States is polarized. According to Fiorina and his coauthors in *Culture War? The Myth of a Polarized America*, it is not the average American who has become more polarized over the past several decades, but rather political elites: "A polarized political class," they write, "makes the citizenry *appear* [emphasis added] polarized, but it is largely that—an appearance."[8]

One reason Fiorina's argument makes sense is that, hearkening back to Converse, the average American simply isn't ideologically sophisticated or developed enough to exhibit the kind of polarization that ought to trouble observers of American democracy and political institutions. Instead, Fiorina believes that while certain issues or debates in American politics—such as abortion and gun rights—do attract loud voices from the polarized fringes, the data shows that most people are not particularly extreme on

---

6. Without getting too technical, NOMINATE scores allow researchers to compare ideology among members of Congress over time. We can therefore know precisely how ideologically comparable Senator Ted Cruz in 2020 and, say, Senator Mark Hatfield in 1980 are, telling us how two important Republican senators differ in their conservatism. This lets scholars make observations about the ideological trajectory of (and changes within) American political institutions, backed up by more than just anecdotes.

7. Wood, "Elite and Mass Polarization, 1970–2020."

8. Fiorina, Abrams, and Pope, *Culture War?*

these issues. Though the average person may have certain views or ideas about what, say, abortion policy should look like, Fiorina argues these views do not align with the minority of the country that has been polarized on abortion.

It is hard to deny the role of polarization in explaining the current state of American politics. Even if people like Fiorina are right that the average person's attitudes are not particularly polarized, the fact that America's political class—including elected officials, candidates, media personalities, and more—is polarized in important ways carries significant implications for the long-term health of the American political experiment. In reviewing the landscape of research on polarization, *New York Times* columnist Thomas Edsall writes, "Polarization has created its own vicious circle, weeding out moderates, fostering extremists and constraining government action even in times of crisis."[9] And while the average person does lack a strong ideology in the way Converse imagined in 1964, the following section shows how this has led to a concerning development in how we approach politics and civic engagement.

Social Polarization and Sorting

What happens when you cross a population not bound by cohesive ideology or policy preferences with competitive political parties? While this may sound like the setup to a confusing joke, the answer is not funny in the least. Absent constrained ideologies and grounded policy preferences, partisan polarization is bound to be tied to frenetic news cycles, shifting commitments, and opportunistic officials. Polarization of the sort envisioned by the 1950 APSA report may be useful for a functional government under our Constitution, but this is not the kind of polarization we have today.

Lilliana Mason's fascinating book *Uncivil Agreement: How Politics Became Our Identity* helps explain why. Mason, a political scientist researching political behavior and psychology, begins her book with a description of a famous psychological experiment centered on group identity. The "Robbers Cave Experiment," as it came to be known, highlighted the experience of two nearly identical groups of boys brought to neighboring camps in Oklahoma. Despite having little to fight about—the boys all came from similar social backgrounds, were of similar intelligence levels, shared a religious

---

9. Edsall, "We Can't Even Agree on What Is Tearing Us Apart."

identity, etc.—the two groups quickly became adversarial. The driver of this conflict was not athleticism or creative ability, but simply group identity.

Throughout her book, Mason draws important parallels between the Robbers Cave Study and contemporary trends in political polarization. She notes that while Republicans and Democrats eventually took up distinct policy positions (as APSA recommended), they also distinguished themselves on identity. "Being a Republican" carried a different meaning than "being a Democrat." This, combined with Americans' general lack of ideological consistency, paved the way for people to adopt party labels in a way that was both strong and malleable—strong in the sense that people do not regularly change their party identification, but malleable in the sense that people's positions on policies can quickly adjust to changes in their preferred party. It turns out people are more likely to change their minds regarding policies before changing their party affiliation.[10]

This kind of political polarization, Mason notes, is evidence of broader social polarization. Just as Americans are more politically polarized today than in the 1950s, so too is the country more socially polarized. Take something as trivial as television, where multiple surveys show that Republicans and Democrats are consuming not only different news sources, but different shows of all kinds. Mason cites a study from TiVo that sorted programs by popularity among viewers of both parties; a total of zero shows appeared on both lists.[11] "Even when we sit down to watch TV," she writes, "Democrats and Republicans are different kinds of people. Increasingly, we cannot even connect at the water cooler to discuss last night's shows."[12]

Referencing an article from *New York Times* writer Thomas Edsall on how polarization aids campaigns in targeting prospective voters, Mason continues:

> [Democrats and Republicans] receive news from different sources (Democrats like the *Washington Post*, Republicans like the *Washington Times*); they eat at different restaurants (Democrats like Chuck E. Cheese's, Republicans like Macaroni Grill); they drive different cars (Democrats like hybrids, Republicans like Land

---

10. An excellent example of this phenomenon is the Republican Party's shift on trade issues. In 1994, Congress ratified the North American Free Trade Agreement with majority Republican support. Less than twenty-five years later, however, it was Republicans pushing for major changes to NAFTA's free trade framework in response to Donald Trump's populist economic policies.

11. Mason, *Uncivil Agreement*.

12. Mason, *Uncivil Agreement*, 43.

Rovers); they drink different alcohol (Democrats like Cognac, Republicans like Amstel Light). These are culture differences so notable that campaigns rely on them to target advertising at the voters they are most likely to attract.[13]

Importantly, all these forms of social polarization end up strengthening political polarization, given our tendency to consolidate our identities into homogenous buckets.[14] If we spend more and more of our time with people who resemble ourselves in many important ways, we are encountering different kinds of people less and less. This can even be seen in our church families—according to author Jeff Bilbro, "We are in danger of developing a greater sense of camaraderie with those who laugh at Peter Sagal's jokes or get their news from Anderson Cooper than with members of church who happen to vote for the wrong political party."[15]

Writing for the American Values Coalition, Ian McLoud identifies the consequences of this kind of sorting for the American political experiment:

> For a pluralistic society like America to work, we need different people with different views and ideas to help point out where we are blind. The problem with Americans choosing to self-sort into like-minded communities is that we will lose the ability to see our blind spots and eventually understand that we are blind.[16]

Unfortunately, as Mason notes in *Uncivil Agreement* (and as Bill Bishop details in *The Big Sort*[17]), this is precisely what has been happening. And, as the following section shows, there are far bigger consequences than what we watch on television.

Negative Partisanship, Schadenfreude, and Violence

Polarization has consequences beyond the explicitly political. Research from the American Enterprise Institute found that right- and left-leaning Americans both reported they had stopped talking to a friend or family member because of political disagreements.[18] And while this research found

13. Mason, *Uncivil Agreement*, 44.
14. Mason and Wronski, "One Tribe to Bind Them All."
15. Bilbro, *Reading the Times*, 144.
16. McLoud, "Why Our Neighborhoods Are Becoming More Partisan."
17. Bishop, *Big Sort*.
18. Abrams, "Polarization in American Family Life Is Overblown."

this behavior more common among liberals, another study confirmed that people of all political stripes are affected; "Anger and social polarization," wrote an author of this study, "are bipartisan phenomena."[19] This shouldn't be surprising to Christians, given our knowledge of sin and the resulting temptation to dismiss people made in God's image, but that doesn't make it any less discouraging.

Another consequence of polarization is a breakdown in social trust. According to philosophy professor Kevin Vallier, since the 1970s the level of social trust in America—the idea that strangers will respect and abide by established norms, political and otherwise—has dropped precipitously, with less than a third of Americans today believing that most people can be trusted.[20] And while this development does carry expressly political implications, it also speaks to a larger erosion of American social norms. This is consistent with Robert Putnam's cataloging of the decline in social capital in America, exemplified in his landmark book *Bowling Alone*.[21]

But what specifically is driving these declining levels of social trust and increasing tendencies toward alienation from those with whom we disagree? One explanation is *negative partisanship*, which describes people aligning *against* one political party instead of affiliating *with* one. Under negative partisanship, people care more about beating their opponents and less about enacting meaningful policies. Rather than ideology acting to inform policymaking and civic engagement, negative partisanship explains how ideology—consistent with Mason's research on social polarization—simply helps us figure out who our enemies are.

In July 2021, *Politico* reporter Erin Banco visited Sheffield, Alabama for a story on its residents' hesitation concerning COVID-19 vaccines amidst surging cases. Recalling conversations with area doctors, nurses, and others, Banco highlighted a message of frustration and exhaustion that more people had not received the vaccine. The reason? Anger stemming from the results of the 2020 election. "Many people here," Banco wrote, "are turning down COVID-19 vaccines because they are angry that President Donald Trump lost the election and sick of Democrats in Washington thinking they know what's best."[22] This brings to mind the joke of the man repeatedly stabbing himself in the foot and being asked if it hurt, only to respond,

---

19. Webster, "Anger and Social Polarization Are Bipartisan Phenomena."
20. Vallier, "Why Are Americans So Distrustful of Each Other?"
21. Putnam, *Bowling Alone*.
22. Banco, "In Alabama and Louisiana, Partisan Opposition to Vaccine Surges."

"Yeah, but liberals *hate* it." You can swap "liberals" for "conservatives" and the message remains the same: Negative partisanship drives people to do inexplicable things in the name of "owning" their opponents.

Research is clear about the influence of negative partisanship on political behavior. In a 2018 article, political scientists Alan Abramowitz and Steven Webster show that negative partisanship has become a steady presence in American politics since the 1980s, leading to greater party loyalty and less split-ticket voting. This phenomenon was tested in 2016 with a presidential election featuring historically unpopular nominees, but "the data suggests that partisans were still overwhelmingly likely to vote for their own party's candidates."[23] Moreover, over the past few decades Republicans' and Democrats' views toward their own parties have remained essentially unchanged, but their opposition to the other party has noticeably increased.[24]

Negative partisanship portends problems for the future of the American political system. When voting, people have historically used retrospective logic when evaluating candidates and options. That is, we have generally looked to past performance to inform how we will vote in the next election. For example, if one party is in control of government, and the current situation is bleak, then that party should expect to be punished in the next election. Nobody highlighted this perspective better than Ronald Reagan in his 1980 presidential campaign, when, during his sole debate with President Jimmy Carter, Reagan looked into the camera and asked the American people: "Are you better off than you were four years ago?"

Negative partisanship upends this process. Instead of evaluating elected officials on performance and holding them responsible (positively or negatively) for recent events, negative partisanship encourages people to focus instead on what would make their opponents the angriest. These kinds of attitudes are reasonable when, say, rooting against a sports team or athlete you dislike, but not when making political decisions that shape our society, advocating policies that affect our communities, and pursuing justice in the name of truly loving our neighbors.

The German language famously includes words that are difficult to translate, expressing feelings or emotions without parallel in other languages. A well-known example is the word *schadenfreude*, which loosely translates to "taking pleasure in the misfortunate of others." Steven Webster has

23. Abramowitz and Webster, "Negative Partisanship."
24. Blue, "Rise of Negative Partisanship and How It Drives Voters."

researched this idea in American politics, finding that people's attitudes on a variety of policy issues, including health care and taxation, are influenced by schadenfreude. Additionally, his research finds "a sizable portion of the American public is more likely than not to vote for candidates who promise to pass policies that 'disproportionately harm' supporters of the opposing political party," and establishes that a demand for cruel candidates is highest among those exhibiting high levels of schadenfreude.[25]

Even if you hadn't considered the role that schadenfreude plays in American politics, odds are you've seen it in action. Consider the social media environment any time a prominent elected official makes a mistake or suffers defeat; that official's opponents are prone to celebrate his or her misfortune. My favorite example of schadenfreude in action comes from 2009, when a conservative group reacted with laughter and applause when learning that the United States would not be hosting the 2016 Olympic Games. Why such joy at a loss for the country? Because President Barack Obama, their main opponent at the time, had traveled to Denmark to lobby for Chicago, his hometown, to be chosen as the host city.[26]

Finding joy in the misfortunate of others, especially those with whom you deeply disagree, is among the basest of human conditions. It also poses real challenges to American politics: taken to its logical end, partisan schadenfreude—like its cousin, negative partisanship—means refusing to consider voting for a candidate from the "other" party no matter who "your" party gets behind, regardless of past performance or what "your" candidate believes in. Keeping the opposition from victory and adding to their misery becomes more important than anything else.

These attitudes and practices may strike the reader as childish and harmful; indeed, they should! But they are not the worst development to come from an increasingly polarized political environment. In *Radical American Partisanship*, political scientists Nathan Kalmoe and Lilliana Mason explore the linkages between political partisanship and the tendency toward endorsing or justifying violence against one's political opponents.[27] Their results are equal parts troubling and, for those of us paying attention, unsurprising: In 2017, 60 percent of people surveyed said the opposing party represented a "serious threat to the United States," while four in 10 people said their political opponents "are not just worse for politics—they

---

25. Webster, Glynn, and Motta, "Partisan Schadenfreude and Candidate Cruelty."
26. Thrush, "Basking in Olympic Snub Risky for GOP."
27. Kalmoe and Mason, *Radical American Partisanship*.

are downright evil."[28] When people view their political opponents in these terms, employing violence against them isn't that outlandish of an idea; in fact, given the perceived stakes, violence could be a justified necessity.

Kalmoe and Mason also find that partisan Democrats *and* Republicans are susceptible to endorsing violence; it is not a problem relegated to just one of our major parties, even if Republicans have exhibited a higher tendency since the candidacy of Donald Trump. This tracks with what we have seen in practice. The violence at the US Capitol on January 6, 2021 was led primarily by political conservatives and Republicans upset with the outcome of the 2020 presidential election, at then-President Trump's urging. And the violence and vandalism directed at pro-life pregnancy centers in 2022 was organized by Far Left groups opposed to the US Supreme Court's decision that overturned *Roe v. Wade*'s guarantee for a constitutional right to abortion.[29] For the people in both of these camps, introducing violence into the political realm was a justified—even necessary—expression of their different grievances.

What can be done to stem this tide? Kalmoe and Mason suggest that political elites have an important role to play. In one survey experiment, the researchers gave respondents statements attributed to major political figures denouncing violence and measured whether these statements affected people's support for violence. They found that "top party leaders can significantly reduce partisan vilification and approval of violence among partisans with their pacifying messages."[30] But given the polarization we've observed and the lack of electoral incentives to oppose extreme rhetoric, this solution is far from guaranteed. The likelier scenario, at least in the short term, is for support for violence to grow alongside schadenfreude and negative partisanship, with those on the fringes of both political parties continuing to dominate how we think about—and how we vilify—our political opponents.

FINAL THOUGHTS ON POLARIZATION

What does this mean for us as followers of Christ? Earlier in this chapter I said Christians are just as susceptible to polarization as anyone else; there aren't studies finding that self-described Christians are any less likely to be

---

28. Kalmoe and Mason, *Radical American Partisanship*, 44.
29. *Dobbs v. Jackson Women's Health Organization*, 597 U.S. ___.
30. Kalmoe and Mason, *Radical American Partisanship*, 149.

prone to polarization. In fact, one study found that people are increasingly polarized on religious lines when it comes to central cultural issues like abortion and LGBTQ rights.[31] The bottom line is political and social polarization is real, it is ugly, and it is getting worse. And given where our hope lies as Christians, how polarization affects us in our political engagement is an important question.

Writing for *Mere Orthodoxy*, Patrick Pierson laments the state of "dogmatic partisanship" in American politics and, by extension, Christians' participation in this system.[32] It isn't that partisanship is bad; after all, factions of the sort envisioned by James Madison in *Federalist 10* are inevitable, and, properly conceived, give rise to compromise necessary in a pluralist system like ours. No, it is the negative aspects of polarization that are so troubling for America's political future. "Soon enough," Pierson writes,

> We will realize that our present approach to public life leaves us in a precarious position reminiscent of early 20th century trench warfare—either hunker down with your comrades only to be wasted by disease and sickness, or poke your head out and fall prey to the intermittent fire of enemy snipers. In time, political polarization creates an impervious no-man's-land from which no one escapes unscathed.

Concluding, Pierson asks, "Do we really want to live this way?"

At the same time, our political parties have slowly but steadily drifted to their extreme ends, virtually guaranteeing Pierson's trench warfare analogy. Republicans, author Bonnie Kristian says, have abandoned the politics of Reagan and Bush for something else entirely: "Instead of prudence, profligacy. Instead of serious politics, entertainment. Instead of virtue, victory. The change is so significant I'm rarely willing to use the word 'conservative' to talk about the American right, because so little of it is conservative at all."[33] Democrats, meanwhile, have grown more extreme in their rhetoric and policies on abortion, gender and sexuality, and religious freedom.[34] For

---

31. Castle and Stepp, "Partisanship, Religion, and Issue Polarization."
32. Pierson, "Dogmatic Partisanship's Dead End."
33. Kristian, "2 Decades of Right Turns."
34. The Democratic Party's extremism on abortion rights is a major departure from the "Safe, legal, and rare" rhetoric of the Clinton years, while the party's support for the Equality Act and its dismissal of religious exemptions in the domain of LGBTQ rights is a far cry from their near-unanimous support for 1993's Religious Freedom Restoration Act.

Christians tasked with making imperfect choices in our electoral decision making, these choices are starker than ever.

On the one hand, it isn't shocking to see our society approach politics and culture this way. These are important questions with important stakes, and in a society less tethered to a Christian worldview than it has ever been, idols of all kinds will invariably rise up to take its place. We can, in a sense, expect our society to be enraptured by our current moment of political and social polarization. But as Christians, we who are in the world but not of it, what exactly is our excuse? If our political engagement is indistinguishable from the world's, then we are failing in our calling to be both salt and light to a world desperately in need. And while Christians are unlikely to reform our political climate single-handedly, we can, at the very least, push back and model a different—and far, far better—kind of political engagement (more on this in chapter 4).

While troubling and tempting, political polarization and its progeny of negative partisanship, schadenfreude, and violence are not the only challenges Christians will face as we seek to shape our world through political engagement. Just as American politics is amid a decades-long transformation, so too is culture in general. It is to these related yet distinct shifts we now turn.

3

The Culture Shift

"Christians are actually being persecuted in America."[1]

In my experience, few questions ruffle as many feathers as whether America was founded as a Christian nation. Two contradictory and passionate perspectives quickly emerge. On the one side are those who believe the United States and its founders were primarily influenced largely by principles of the European Enlightenment, not those from Christianity or the Bible.[2] As evidence they offer the deist views of certain influential founders—including Thomas Jefferson and Benjamin Franklin—and cite the Establishment Clause of the First Amendment, as well as the fact that the Constitution does not directly reference or allude to God at any point. The obvious conclusion, they reason, is that the United States was decidedly not founded as a Christian nation and should not be guided by Christian principles today.

On the other side are those who believe that the new nation was clearly influenced and inspired by Christianity in its founding. They will point to quotations and passages from founding debates referencing Christianity, God, and related terms and language. One advocate of such a view is David Barton. While not a historian by training or credentials, Barton has written several books and dozens of essays arguing for an explicitly Christian American founding. He cites passages from the Constitution he

---

1. Wolfe, "Christians Actually Are Being Persecuted in America."
2. See, for example, Seidel, *Founding Myth*.

THE CULTURE SHIFT

claims are lifted, verbatim, from the Bible.³ He goes so far as to suggest academic historians are involved in a conspiracy to obscure the religious beliefs and motivations of the country's founders.⁴ Barton and others like him conclude that the creation of America was an unequivocally Christian one, with major implications for contemporary debates over law and policy.

The actual answer to this question is almost certainly more nuanced. Consider Mark David Hall's book *Did America Have a Christian Founding?*⁵ Hall, a professor of politics and expert on the American founding, persuasively argues that while the founders did not envision their new nation to be a theocratic regime commanding religious commitment from its citizens, they nevertheless would have been supportive of Christianity—and religion in general—when structuring the new system of government. While America was not meant to be a Christian nation legally speaking, Hall argues, it was nevertheless meant to be a nation where religion would be encouraged to flourish as a necessary component of pluralist republican democracy.⁶ While the United States may not have been designed to be a formal Christian nation, that does not mean Christianity was never meant to have a prominent role in the nation's DNA.

Whether the United States was founded to be a Christian nation is not just a matter for historical debate. It matters because of its relevance to ongoing observations about the condition of American culture. Consider the claim at the top of this chapter from commentator William Wolfe. Included as part of a lengthier statement on Twitter, Wolfe argued that Christians face persecution in America today, despite calls to the contrary from skeptical others, including other Christians.⁷ Specifically, Wolfe—who also served in the Department of Defense during the Trump administration—cited instances of business owners facing lawsuits for alleged discrimination,

---

3. Hagerty, "Most Influential Evangelist You've Never Heard Of."
4. Barton, *Original Intent*.
5. Hall, *Did America Have a Christian Founding?*
6. This argument echoes that of the French aristocrat and anthropologist Alexis de Tocqueville. In the early nineteenth century, Tocqueville spent time in the new United States observing its people and customs, ultimately publishing his observations in the seminal *Democracy in America*. While the text has become essential for understanding myriad elements of early American government and constitutional design, Tocqueville's descriptions of the role religious life played in the new nation remains critical to understanding how the United States turned out differently than its revolutionary peers, including France.
7. See, for example, Yancey, "Is There Really Anti-Christian Discrimination in America?"

public employees facing recriminations for supposed public demonstrations of faith, and more. "They are coming for us at every turn," Wolfe wrote, "schools, commerce, in the public square—and they will use every means of power they can to silence us or lock us up."[8]

This talk of persecution is connected to talk of the founding. For some conservative Christians, if the United States strays from its core principles, it cannot function as intended or serve the people it is charged with serving. For these Christians, the fact that we have seen the sorts of conflicts Wolfe outlined above is evidence that the nation has, in fact, strayed. The solution, it follows, must be a return to the country's Christian roots in both the public and private squares. These roots must be seen in laws and judicial opinions handed down from our governmental institutions. Otherwise, Christian citizens will continue to face challenges they were not intended to face while living in the United States of America.

As a result of these arguments, there has been a backlash of sorts from those inherently skeptical of the role of religion—especially Christianity—in the public square. These voices believe that Christians claiming persecution in America today do so primarily as cover for their discriminatory views and harmful behaviors.[9] Observers also point to an alarming increase in Christian nationalism, views that prioritize a very specific kind of Christianity through law and public policy.[10] These observers argue that the challenges Wolfe identifies are not endemic challenges at all but rather simply a result of an increasingly pluralistic and diverse society. They see any cries of persecution as responses to inevitable cultural changes where Christianity may no longer have a privileged place in society.

In this chapter, I try to assess this debate from a dispassionate position. I attempt to make the case that there are, in fact, significant challenges for Christians as we wade further into a transformed and changing American culture. The backlash described above, I argue, is dismissive of real concerns Christians—especially theologically and socially conservative Christians—are facing, or will soon face, in this new landscape. At the same time, I will argue that the fact that these challenges exist does not pose existential risks for Christians and our kingdom witness. Though the landscape of American culture has undoubtedly changed over the last several decades, Christians should not be fearful about our future in it. Our

---

8. Wolfe, "It's a Pitched Battle Right Now."
9. See, for example, Seidel, *American Crusade*.
10. See, for example, Gorski and Perry, *Flag and the Cross*.

confidence ought to come from he who overcame the world while refusing to overthrow its political systems.

Christians will be facing challenges in the years ahead in two major ways. The first is *demographic*, centered on declining religious affiliations, shrinking church attendance, and general changes in the composition of religious traditions. Demographic and empirical analysis show clear changes to American religion, with the political and social polarization of the last chapter playing an important role. The second kind of challenge is harder to describe. It is at once philosophical and psychological, personal and collective. It is a way of seeing the world around us existing primarily to serve *us* rather than seeing the world and its people as in need of being served. I describe this challenge as *ideological*, though it is far deeper than mere political values and beliefs. It encompasses how we understand and perceive reality.

These two kinds of challenges are undoubtedly related, but they require different responses from Christians seeking to navigate an increasingly complex and challenging cultural environment. It is no longer enough to assume that we share certain foundations about the way the world ought to be. As is the case with political and social polarization, to respond effectively and faithfully to this transformed environment we need to understand what exactly we're up against.

DEMOGRAPHIC CHALLENGES

To say that the United States is experiencing seismic demographic changes is an understatement. Consider data on the racial makeup of the country: According to Census data and major demographic studies, by 2044 the United States will be a majority-minority country, meaning that there will be more non-white people in the US than white people.[11] Objectively, this is neither good nor bad, but it is certainly a huge milestone in American history. Research clearly shows the role race plays in political behavior, in terms of voting, trust in government, and support for certain policies. These shifts will inevitably lead to changes in how the country's two main political parties seek votes, at least in terms of the platforms they propose and the kinds of candidates they nominate. Demographics may not be destiny, but they do forebode a changing future for American politics.[12]

---

11. Colby and Ortman, "Projections of the Size and Composition of the U.S. Population."
12. This is to say nothing of the increase in multiracial population, which promises

At the same time, the United States is undergoing significant changes in religious demographics, with similar implications not just for political behavior but for the shape and contours of American culture altogether. For most of American history, to be American was to be Christian—specifically, Protestant. Even among non-Christians today, there remains an association between American identity and Christianity.[13] Until relatively recently, to identify as something other than a Christian in many parts of the nation would be opening oneself up to scrutiny and questioning. Yes, the First Amendment grants constitutional protections for religious exercise, including for religious minorities, but that is simply the law; culturally, being a Christian has always been the safest choice.[14]

We see remnants of this phenomenon in multiple contexts today. For example, according to the Public Religion Research Institute (PRRI), in 2020 approximately 70 percent of Americans identified as Christian, including evangelicals, Mainline Protestants, Catholics, and Black Protestants.[15] But among representatives and senators of the 117th Congress (spanning 2021–2022), that percentage was nearly 90 percent.[16] Similarly, in 2020, 23 percent of Americans were unaffiliated with a religion, compared to just one—one!—member of Congress. There are myriad explanations for this, but one is that those seeking higher office find it beneficial to highlight religious convictions to draw potential voters. Even as the cultural tide has begun to turn, members of Congress still find usefulness in appeals to religion, especially Christianity.

But the cultural tide *is* turning. While Christians (broadly defined) remain the largest religious group in the United States, the number of Christians as a proportion of the country's religious landscape has been trending downward for decades. Research from the Pew Research Center shows the number of Americans identifying as Christian has decreased by over 10 percent in just over a decade.[17] Among them, those describing themselves as "born-again or evangelical" outnumber those who do

---

to shake up the status quo of American politics in other ways. See Alba, Levy, and Myers, "Myth of a Majority-Minority America."

13. Jacobs and Theis-Morse, "Belonging in a 'Christian Nation.'"

14. Of course, there are exceptions here, with the Black church and Catholic community notable among them.

15. Public Religion Research Institute, "2020 Census of American Religion."

16. Pew Research Center, "Faith on the Hill."

17. Pew Research Center, "In U.S., Decline of Christianity Continues at Rapid Pace."

not, suggesting that while Christianity in general is shrinking in the United States, evangelicalism is shrinking slower than its Mainline Protestant counterparts.[18] And though research from PRRI finds that this decline may have stabilized in the early 2020s, there is nothing to suggest Christianity is preparing to surge back to the place it once held in religion and American public life.[19]

In addition to changes in religious affiliation, over the last several decades the United States has seen a steady decline in other important markers of religious behavior. Pew finds that Americans attending religious services regularly (defined as monthly or more) has dropped consistently since 2007, while people who attend a few times a year or less now make up most of the population.[20] In 2020, less than half of Americans reported being a member of a religious congregation, down over 20 percent in two decades.[21] And Americans are praying less than they used to, with less than half saying they pray daily and nearly a third saying they seldom or never pray.[22] By nearly any measure, Americans are not just identifying as less Christian and less religious than previous generations; their actions are following suit.

Religious decline is most pronounced among younger Americans. Consider millennials, who, by 2019, were "almost as likely to say they have no religion as they are to identify as Christian."[23] Not only that, but according to research from Daniel Cox and the American Enterprise Institute, the way young Americans experience religion is dramatically different compared to their older neighbors. Consider this:

> Young adults today have had entirely different religious and social experiences than previous generations did. The parents of millennials and Generation Z did less to encourage regular participation in formal worship services and model religious behaviors in their children than had previous generations. Many childhood religious

---

18. Smith, "About Three-in-Ten U.S. Adults Are Now Religiously Unaffiliated."
19. Sullivan, "Proportion of White Christians In The U.S. Has Stopped Shrinking."
20. Pew Research Center, "In U.S., Decline of Christianity Continues at Rapid Pace."
21. Jones, "U.S. Church Membership Falls Below Majority for First Time." One reason for this decline may be the rise of churches not emphasizing membership for regular attenders, such as nondenominational or large, multi-site churches. Nevertheless, the decline is stark.
22. Blair, "Fewer than Half of American Adults Pray Daily."
23. Cox and Thomson-DeVeaux, "Millennials Are Leaving Religion."

activities that were once common . . . have become more of the exception than the norm.²⁴

This research offers little encouragement to those predicting a resurgence of Christianity within the status quo. "There is little evidence to suggest that Americans who have disaffiliated will ever return," Cox writes. "Disaffiliated Americans express significant skepticism about the societal benefits of religion, even more than those who have never identified with a religious tradition." As more and more younger Americans leave religion—and Christianity—behind, we can expect few of them to come back.

When you separate Christians by tradition—evangelicals, Catholics, and the like—no one single group is larger than "the nones," those saying they are atheist, agnostic, or "nothing in particular." Though Christianity remains the single largest religion in the United States, the nones are by far the country's fastest growing community. The nones, on average, tend to be on the lower end of the socioeconomic spectrum. They are more likely to be men, young, nonwhite, and childless, and more likely to identify as Democrats than Republicans.²⁵

Ryan Burge is an expert on the nones and their increasing prominence in American religion. In his book *The Nones*, Burge explains the phenomenon of increasing religious disaffiliation in the United States.²⁶ He clarifies that while atheists and agnostics—those who say they don't believe in God or question whether God exists, respectively—have historically dominated discussion about the nones, the "nothing in particular" group is far more consequential to the future of American religion and culture. Crucially, the "nothing in particulars," according to Burge, "appear to be a growing segment of society that is 'checked out.'"²⁷ They are not intellectually opposed to God; instead, they are, for one reason or another, simply disinterested.

These demographic changes pose significant challenges for Christians navigating our cultural and political environments. First—and this is a challenge for American society, too—the decline of Christianity and institutional religion inevitably affects the production of *social capital*, the ties that bind us together. For social scientist Robert Putnam, declining social capital in the US was exemplified by an odd phenomenon: in the

---

24. Cox, "Generation Z and the Future of Faith in America."
25. Public Religion Research Institute, "2020 Census of American Religion."
26. Burge, *Nones*.
27. Burge, "Rise of the 'nothing in Particulars' May Be Sign."

early 1990s Americans were bowling at rates commensurate with previous generations, yet the number of bowling leagues had decreased over several decades.[28] Why? Because Americans were doing more individually and less collectively; still active, but more and more isolated. Technological alienation via social media, while bringing with it the *appearance* of togetherness, has only driven this dearth of social capital. In perhaps our era's greatest irony, our capacity for connectedness has never been greater, but we have never been more alone.

Religion is just one producer of social capital—along with civic organizations, sports leagues, and hobby associations—but it has been a major one. Without religion (and, historically, Christianity) to cultivate and incubate social capital, people will not have the same opportunities to connect and meet others different from them. As social capital disappears, so too does civic engagement and participation. And as civic engagement and participation decline, so too does trust in our institutions and one another. Timothy Carney puts it this way:

> Americans are less attached to society, their neighbors, their communities, other humans. Lacking the environment of a strong community, more Americans lack the scaffolding to climb above their starting point. More Americans lack the support structure that they would need to build a family. More Americans lack role models, and they lack *roles*. They are displaced persons living in their home country, even in their native state or hometown. They are strangers in their own land.[29]

Think of social capital as the deep webbing underlying our American identity. When this webbing erodes, so too do our essential connections to one another, and the health of our political system—and our society in general—with them.

The decline of Christianity is also fueling a rise in political polarization between the religious and nonreligious. To be sure, there have always been differences between, say, Christians and non-Christians when it comes to partisanship and political behavior, but these differences have always had their outliers and exceptions. Lately, these differences have exacerbated, as religious conservatives (and particularly Christians) are increasingly finding a political home in the Republican Party, while secular Americans are

---

28. Putnam, *Bowling Alone*.
29. Carney, *Alienated America*, 93.

increasingly affiliating with the Democratic Party.[30] Pew data adds interesting wrinkles to this, finding that Americans are also politically sorted based on whether they believe in God, how often they pray, and whether they look to religion for guidance on moral questions.[31]

Moreover, though Christianity has declined as a share of the population, the percentage of "highly religious" Americans has remained steady. This, combined with the growing share of the country who are unaffiliated with religion, guarantees conflict in both culture and politics. "Only in the United States," three researchers wrote, "do these two groups [the highly religious and the secular] have to deal with each other on somewhat equal grounds."[32] I will argue in chapter 5 that pluralism is undoubtedly a good thing for Christians tasked with the Great Commission; persuasion is superior to coercion. Factions and conflict in political society are better than unanimity and groupthink. But we must be prepared to accept the messiness that comes with it.

Relatedly, Michele Margolis details a troubling trend in *From Politics to the Pews*: Americans are increasingly choosing churches based on their political commitments.[33] This contradicts much of what social scientists thought we knew about the relationship between religion and politics—namely, that *religion* affects *politics*—but her data and arguments are compelling. Margolis's findings are consistent with what she calls a "life cycle theory" of religious participation, where people are socialized into religion as children, "rebel" during adolescence, and either do or do not return to religious communities during adulthood. While this is happening, their political attitudes are forming and stabilizing, meaning that if they return to religion as adults, their political views inevitably influence their choice of congregation.

The levers of American government may be hastening these conflicts, too. According to a study from Paul Djupe and Jacob Neiheisel, certain US Supreme Court decisions have furthered divides between those—especially the religiously unaffiliated—who support same-sex marriage and gay rights and those—especially conservative Christians—who do not. More importantly, these decisions have affected local churches, with tensions among parishioners leading to changes in the political composition

30. Smith, "More White Americans Adopted than Shed Evangelical Label."
31. Pew Research Center, "Religious Landscape Study."
32. James, Boyd, and Carroll, "Why the Partisan Divide?"
33. Margolis, *From Politics to the Pews*.

of these churches. "Some," they write, "may initially draw down their attendance at religious services, while others may leave for a more hospitable environment or fall from the faith altogether. The functional result will be an increase in the number of nones and greater sorting along both religious and political lines."[34] Christians cannot avoid engaging and participating in our communities, and these increasingly polarized dynamics will only make our efforts more difficult.

Finally, we as Christians can no longer take for granted being in an environment inherently warm to our faith. For most of American history, Christians have existed in a position of cultural dominance, being able to benefit from certain things that Christians living in other parts of the world never have. As a white Christian, I have never feared for my safety venturing out for Sunday morning worship, nor have I been concerned about being listed as a potential enemy of the state because of my faith. For all the concern over corporate bias against Christianity, each year major stores—including Target, Walmart, and, of course, Hobby Lobby—display aisles and aisles of decorations and accessories relating to the two most important days of the Christian calendar: Easter and Christmas. It has been, all things considered, pretty easy to be a Christian in the United States.

As our culture continues to evolve demographically, the status quo will no doubt change with it. This does not mean American Christians should prepare for state-sanctioned persecution akin to that in Saudi Arabia or North Korea. But it does mean that the act of professing Christianity—in thought, word, and deed—will no longer be culturally protected as it has been for most of the country's history. In a widely discussed essay for the journal *First Things*, Aaron Renn separated the history of American Christianity into three "worlds"—the positive, the neutral, and the negative.[35] In the positive world, Renn argues, Christianity was seen as essential to the country's flourishing and success. In the neutral world, Christianity was seen as one of many valuable religious and philosophical traditions woven into the American tapestry.

But in our current negative world—which, according to Renn, we entered into around 2014—Christianity is seen with suspicion, if not derision. In the negative world, he writes, "Christian morality is expressly repudiated and seen as a threat to the public good and the new public moral order.

---

34. Djupe and Neiheisel, "How Future Supreme Court Rulings May Fuel the Decline of Religion."

35. Renn, "Three Worlds of Evangelicalism."

Subscribing to Christian moral views or violating the secular moral order brings negative consequences." I will return to Renn's "three worlds" framework in chapter 5, as there is plenty to critique and push back against in his story. For now, though, it is a useful tool to think through changes in how our culture has encountered and understood the Christian faith, particularly in terms of how Christianity necessarily influences the public square.

IDEOLOGICAL CHALLENGES

The above demographic challenges will be difficult enough for Christians to navigate in the years ahead. American culture is objectively changing, and we, as the body of Christ, must be aware of these changes to best reach and transform the culture for the kingdom of God. But there are subtler, deeper, and more foundational changes underway than simple changes to our collective composition. These changes are largely ideological and internalized and are, therefore, more difficult to see and less easily confronted. While demographics provide their own set of challenges, these ideological challenges are harder to reckon with.

In his 1984 book *The Great Evangelical Disaster*, Francis Schaeffer minced no words on what these ideological challenges meant for the state of American culture: "Our culture has been squandered and lost, and largely thrown away. Indeed, to call it a moral breakdown puts it mildly. Morality itself has been turned on its head with every form of moral perversion being praised and glorified in the media and the world of entertainment."[36] Schaeffer points to abortion and disregard for human life as one indicator, but also cites other cultural changes—such as increasing divorce rates, including among evangelicals—as evidence of this disaster.[37]

Schaeffer was not pleased in assessing Christians' responses to the new reality of a lost culture. "Sadly," he wrote, "we must say that very few Christians have understood the battle that we are in."[38] One major reason for this, he argued, is how evangelicals have interpreted—or, in some cases, ignored—the Bible as it pertains to our views on public policy: "God's word," he wrote, "has many times been allowed to be bent, to conform to the surrounding, passing, changing culture of that moment rather than to

---

36. Schaeffer, *Great Evangelical Disaster*, 20.
37. Schaeffer, *Great Evangelical Disaster*, 63.
38. Schaeffer, *Great Evangelical Disaster*, 23.

stand as the inerrant word of God . . ."[39] Schaeffer said we see this with Christians who find reasons to equivocate on abortion and human life, and we see it with Christians who dismiss scriptural commands pertaining to refugees and immigrants. We must infer that Schaeffer, were he alive today, would have a similar (if not more pessimistic) diagnosis about how Christians approach our present cultural challenges.

Carl Trueman's *The Rise and Triumph of the Modern Self*, published thirty-six years after *The Great Evangelical Disaster*, is a terrific source for making sense of these emerging ideological shifts in American—and, more broadly, Western—culture.[40] Trueman is a theologian and church historian, but his most recent work has been to critique the trend toward individualism in Western thought, both outside and inside the church. Specifically, Trueman critiques the growth of *expressive individualism*—the idea that one's ultimate identity and value is found in the expression of their truest, deepest self. At first glance and as far as ideologies go, this may not sound particularly insidious. After all, do we not tell our kids to be true to who they are, to not conform to the disordered expectations of the world? What, precisely, is the harm in encouraging people to be themselves?

The problem with expressive individualism is in its ordering of things. Tracing developments in philosophy and psychology over the past century, Trueman concludes that expressive individualism is not sufficiently rooted beyond a person's preferences, priming the pump for relativism and contradicting the first question and answer of the Heidelberg Catechism:

> Q: What is your only comfort in life and death?
> A: That I am not my own, but belong—body and soul, in life and in death—to my faithful Savior, Jesus Christ.[41]

When we anchor who we are in our fallen and malleable preferences, what follows, according to Trueman, is chaos. He draws heavily on Sigmund Freud's influence on contemporary discussions of identity and sexuality, and also on thinkers like Karl Marx and Friedrich Nietzsche and their influence on economics and power. These perspectives, Trueman writes, "[make] human nature and all that depends on such a notion to be functions of the economic structure of society. That makes human nature a

---

39. Schaeffer, *Great Evangelical Disaster*, 65.
40. Trueman, *Rise and Triumph of the Modern Self*.
41. Reformed Church in America, "Heidelberg Catechism."

plastic thing, subject to historical change as the economic dynamics of society change."[42]

We see these influences all around us. Though it is true that *all* politics is, to some extent, identity politics, our society's increasing emphasis on and deferral to a person's identity as the apex of authority is striking. "Living one's truth" is a mantra for well-being and self-actualization, emphasizing an individual's perception of reality over objective reality. How one *feels* about something matters just as much as whether said thing is real.[43] Of course, this isn't *just* about using correct pronouns, though it is emblematic of the phenomenon. And if someone's identity or point of view—their *truth*—is challenged or seen as mistaken, it may be tantamount to intimidation or even violence.[44]

Christians might see this as a difficult path to tread: Should we defer to respecting the wishes of our neighbors and betray what we are confident is objective truth, or affirm certain truths about human nature and ignore people's claims about their identity and truth systems? These options may not always be mutually exclusive, but they sometimes will be. And this is precisely Trueman's point. Christians living in what philosopher Charles Taylor called "a secular age" will be increasingly pulled in opposite directions—one in which Christ is sovereign over all things, and another in which culture is "preoccupied with the self-actualization and fulfillment of the individual because there is no greater purpose that can be justified in any ultimately authoritative sense."[45] This difficulty is not new—pluralistic societies will always yield competing belief systems—but its recent manifestation is daunting.

Where we can see expressive individualism most evidently today is, according to Trueman, in culture's evolving understanding of sexuality.

---

42. Trueman, *Rise and Triumph of the Modern Self*, 179.

43. These things are often characterized as being connected to the political left in the United States, but they are also apparent on the political right. Consider former Speaker of the House Newt Gingrich speaking to CNN during the 2016 Republican National Convention. In a discussion of crime rates, CNN's anchor pointed out violent crime had been declining across the country, contradicting the Republican Party's messaging during that year's campaign. Gingrich, however, said data and facts mattered less than what people *believed* to be true. "The average American, I will bet you this morning, does not think crime is down, does not think they are safer," Gingrich said, continuing, "As a political candidate, I'll go with how people feel, and I'll let you go with the theoreticians." See Siegel, "Newt Gingrich Exemplifies Just How Unscientific America Is."

44. Hanna et al., "Actually, We Should Not All Use They/Them Pronouns."

45. Trueman, *Rise and Triumph of the Modern Self*, 80.

Trueman argues that the sexual has become predominant in our culture's reading of identity, psychology, and, yes, politics. "The politics that is produced," he writes, "thereby has a distinctive character precisely because the reality that it thinks it is addressing is at base a psychological one. To transform society politically, then, one must transform society sexually and psychologically."[46] When individual identity is central to politics and sexuality is central to identity, these things become inextricable—and for Christians who harbor theological and scriptural concerns about elements of sexual progression, these concerns are tantamount to attacks on individuals.

Consider the US Supreme Court's same-sex marriage decisions, *United States v. Windsor*[47] and *Obergefell v. Hodges*.[48] In describing the court's reasoning in striking down the federal Defense of Marriage Act and various state bans on same-sex marriage, Trueman laments that the court does not recognize "any rational basis for defining marriage as between one man and one woman."[49] Trueman goes on to list several possible "rational" arguments for defending a traditional, one-man-one-woman definition of marriage, including "the overwhelming consensus of tradition" and the importance of procreation.[50] According to Trueman, those holding to this more traditional definition of marriage must adhere to a more evolved definition or face accusations of bigotry—and the legal consequences that follow. This situation points to "an act of cultural hubris whereby the elites of contemporary culture have an apparent monopoly on what can be declared rational."[51] Inevitably, some Christians will have a more difficult time navigating this environment than others.

Returning to the Heidelberg Catechism, Alan Noble's *You Are Not Your Own* further touches on the ideological shifts in our culture and how these pose significant challenges for Christians today. Just as sexuality played significant roles in Trueman's analysis of expressive individualism,

---

46. Trueman, *Rise and Triumph of the Modern Self*, 250.

47. *U.S. v. Windsor*, 570 U.S. 744.

48. *Obergefell v. Hodges*, 576 U.S. 644.

49. Trueman, *Rise and Triumph of the Modern Self*, 309.

50. Though these arguments are certainly grounded in tradition and are rational to those holding them, it does not necessarily follow that they translate into effective *legal* arguments, specifically when weighed against the constitutional arguments of those supporting same-sex marriage—specifically, that marriage equality is required by the Fourteenth Amendment.

51. Trueman, *Rise and Triumph of the Modern Self*, 309.

Noble identifies technology as a primary culprit. Social media allows people to craft a persona that may or may not align with who they really are. We instantly capture and share photos of ourselves and the world around us, cropped and edited to perfection. "Instead of a common good," Noble writes, "we have billions of private goods. The best we can do is join forces with other people with intersecting identities."[52] We combat increasing cultural alienation by creating alternative realities in which we are the idealized, unspoiled versions of ourselves.

Noble argues Christians are just as susceptible to these challenges as our non-Christian neighbors. At first, this seems surprising. After all, shouldn't our experience with death to sin and resurrection in Christ fundamentally change us? Of course. But sanctification is a lifelong process. The temptations and norms of this world remain. Christians are not immune from the pressures of presentation—indeed, I'd wager that in few places is this temptation stronger than our corporate worship together. This doesn't mean there is no authenticity during a Sunday morning church service, but the norms and expectations of our communities can lead us to project incomplete (or even false) ideas of who we truly are. "Good! How are you?" becomes the default answer to inquiries into our well-being, even though the reality may be more complicated. Sunday mornings are no exception, even though, more so than any other moment of our week, they ought to be.

In terms of ongoing cultural changes and their resulting challenges, Noble's depiction of a world centered on the self is concerning. Just as Robert Putnam recognized why the decline of social capital was important for the future of American cultural and political institutions, the exponential growth and omnipresence of technology raise important questions of their own. When we can cultivate our own realities, complete with tailored information about the world ordered neatly to fit our existing preferences, we no longer must wrestle with competing perspectives and conflicting points of view. In other words, we are no longer required to be in a community. And referencing Emile Durkheim, perhaps the father of contemporary sociology, Noble observes, "When societal values rapidly change, including economic values, people lose the ability to clearly evaluate their lives."[53]

Expressive individualism, found through identity or technology, is not the only ideological challenge Christians must reckon with in a quickly

---

52. Noble, *You Are Not Your Own*, 44.
53. Noble, *You Are Not Your Own*, 309.

transforming culture. In an essay for the *New York Times*, Nate Hochman asks, "What comes after the religious right?"[54] Hochman writes as a Republican increasingly concerned with what changes to American religion mean for the future of political conservatism, an ideology that has traditionally been grounded in religion as a foundation for its values and ethos. He explains how "new secular conservatives and the old religious right are bound together in an uneasy partnership to fight the cultural left." The decline of Christianity as a share of the American religious landscape brings political consequences, but also ideological ones.

On the one hand, this new conservatism may appeal to a broader range of potential voters, "many of whom had been put off by the old conservatism's explicitly religious sheen and don't quite see themselves as Republicans yet." Hochman argues this is one explanation for Donald Trump's appeal in 2016: "While the majority of religious conservatives eventually fell in line behind Mr. Trump," he wrote, "the political and cultural energy he represented was primarily a reflection of the nonreligious right." And while Trump may not have been certain Christians' cup of tea, his victories for social conservatives—especially on reorienting the federal courts in a decidedly friendlier direction—are impossible to ignore. This tradeoff will be worth it for many Christians moving forward, especially in the face of a more antagonistic culture.

On the other hand, as the country continues its slow yet steady march toward secularization, Christians may routinely find themselves without a major place at the table of either major party. Democrats are likely to move further left on issues like abortion and religious freedom. At the same time, Republicans are likely to move further right on issues like immigration and social safety net spending. To be sure, conservative Christians may still benefit from Republican Party policies; Hochman writes, "The new cultural conservatism may protect the embattled minority of traditionalist Christians; it will not restore them to their pre-eminent place in public life, as the old religious conservatism hoped to do." But for Christians seeking to engage and positively transform culture, to confound the existing political order and its limited and imperfect options, this new arrangement may not be what we have in mind.

---

54. Hochman, "What Comes After the Religious Right?"

CIVIL RELIGION AND THE FUTURE OF CHRISTIANITY IN AMERICA

For most of American history, Christianity has played a significant role in structuring what social scientists and others have dubbed the nation's *civil religion*. This idea refers to overarching and generally shared ideas about what is essential to the American story. Civil religion, according to the authors of *Religion and Politics in America*,

> tends to emphasize the unique, "blessed" status of the United States among the nations of the world. It inspires in its followers a sense of divinely ordained American patriotism. The quick appearance of Americans flags and signs reading "God Bless America" in the days immediately following the terrorist attacks of September 11, 2001, as well as the national joy at the quick apprehension of the Boston Marathon bombers in April 2013, are among many examples analysts cite to indicate the presence of the civil religion.[55]

Civil religion knows no tradition; "One can be a faithful adherent of one religious tradition," the authors contend, "and simultaneously celebrate the civil religion." But given Christianity's privileged place throughout America's nearly 250-year story, its influence on civil religion cannot be ignored.

Not surprisingly, the concept of American civil religion has transformed in critical ways following the country's various political, religious, and cultural evolution. What has been taken for granted is far more likely to be contested. In a related sense, it is difficult to imagine the national unity we saw following the 9/11 attacks emerging today, even following an equally traumatic event.[56] Similarly, political scientists have often referred to the "rally around the flag" effect in explaining spikes in presidential approval ratings: During times of crises, people are more likely to give the president the benefit of the doubt and express approval for his decision-making. Given our political polarization, this effect—good or bad—is nowhere near as pronounced as it has been. This is just one instance of the ties that previously bound us being loosened.

Similarly, cultural Christianity is, for the reasons described in this chapter, no longer the default for millions of people. The "death of the Bible

---

55. Fowler et al., *Religion and Politics in America*, 25.

56. In her book on social polarization, Lilliana Mason suggested perhaps the only thing that could turn down the temperature on our political divisions would be an alien invasion. Based on what we saw in chapter 2, consider me skeptical that even this would work. Mason, *Uncivil Agreement*.

Belt" may be a good thing for Christianity—for one thing, fewer "Christians in name only" will lead to more chances for renewed evangelism—but it will nevertheless bring real consequences for the daily lives of many of our neighbors. "The decline of the Bible Belt," Andrew Walker writes, "will be met with a redefined common good that will be anything but good for millions of people." What was once the norm in establishing boundaries and setting the agenda is becoming more foreign with every passing year. For the Christians that remain, we must prepare to live as a minority in an increasingly post-Christian country.

But even though these challenges are real and require serious reflection from Christians concerned about responding to them, they do open doors previously unknown to us as Christians in a predominantly Christian culture. When the makeup of our culture changes, so too do our prospects for engaging this culture—and its politics—in innovative and important ways. Put differently, challenges create and illuminate opportunities. It is to these opportunities we can now turn.

4

A Better Political Engagement

"An idol is anything that you turn to and say, 'Save me.'"[1]

When I started teaching at John Brown University, one thing I quickly discovered was the Enneagram. Formally the Enneagram of Personality, the Enneagram is a method of measuring, interpreting, and numbering personality types. Students would regularly ask what my "number" was, and I would consistently disappoint them by having no clue. This disappointment would quickly turn to speculation, however, as students would venture guesses as to my Enneagram number. Eventually, after several months of prodding and pushing, coupled with my wife borrowing an Enneagram book from a friend, I eventually completed an assessment.

I am, it turns out, a Nine. According to the Enneagram Institute, Nines are "accepting, trusting, and stable. They are usually creative, optimistic, and supportive but can also be too willing to go along with others to keep the peace. They want everything to go smoothly and be without conflict, but they can also tend to be complacent, simplifying problems and minimizing anything upsetting." No wonder, as a type, the Nine is called "the Peacemaker."[2] And I must admit, this characterization captures my personality well: I do tend to avoid conflict, I don't like rocking the boat, and I am naturally drawn to easy conversations about, say, sports and movies

---

1. Keller, "An Idol Is Anything That You Turn to and Say, 'Save Me.'"
2. Enneagram Institute, "Type Nine."

than to difficult conversations that lay bare people's deepest and strongest convictions, especially when they are in disagreement.

Which brings me to an important confession: For someone who has made a career of studying and teaching politics, I really don't like politics that much. Yes, I like making sense of institutional development and individual behavior, and I enjoy analyzing legal decisions and arguing for certain kinds of constitutional interpretation over others. But as for the *act* of politics, with its resulting debate, conflict, and desire to win in supposedly zero-sum situations? As a Nine, that makes me uncomfortable. It makes me anxious. It makes me uneasy.

You might feel the same way when it comes to politics. You might feel conflicted about getting too close to politics because of the risks you think it poses to your faith. So much of our public identity as Christians is predicated on being peacemakers, on being loving, on being winsome, on being *nice*. But winsomeness and kindness are biblical virtues; niceness is not. While Jesus does call us to be peacemakers, avoiding conflict is decidedly not a Christian trait. In fact, sometimes our charge to make peace will lead to conflicts of the messiest kind. Sometimes being "nice" by the world's standards isn't what the moment demands—when the prophets rebuked God's people and when Jesus cleansed the temple, niceness wasn't the driving factor.

I mentioned early in this book that I would not provide a list of policy views Christians should adopt to exhibit a distinctly Christian political engagement. Faithful Christians can and do disagree on policy, even while sharing fundamental convictions about justice, caring for orphans and widows, and welcoming the stranger. It's reasonable and expected for some Christians—including large majorities of white evangelicals—to be passionate Republicans and for others—including large majorities of Black Protestants—to be passionate Democrats, and for still others to be passionately dispassionate about party labels and platforms. We should not question the sincerity of someone's faith based on their voting behavior. Our fallen world is imperfect, as are the political choices we are bound to make.

Consistency—what I will later define as maintaining a standard of beliefs and views regardless of context or consequences—often takes a backseat to pursuing in-the-moment victories. Despite repeated opportunities for consistency, too many of Donald Trump's critics were silent regarding problematic areas of the Biden administration, and many of Biden's critics were likewise silent during the Trump years. It is far easier to critique one's opponents than identify the flaws in one's preferred candidate, president, or party. Not surprisingly, consistency of this sort is rarely seen in the politics of this world. Christians, though, are not called to be of the world. Consistency in our beliefs is just one element of a Christian posture in political engagement, one that has the potential to both confound the world and point towards something (indeed, *someone*) far greater.

The first half of this book spoke to the challenges facing Christians as we contemplate how to engage our complicated and fraught cultural environment. The history of Christian political engagement in America shows the difficulties of engaging faithfully and holistically, and recent evolutions in our political and cultural environment only make this tougher. But these challenges also present new opportunities for Christians to do political engagement well, to make affirmative (and, in some instances, countercultural) arguments for our political system, and to invest in and support institutions essential for the Christian community in an increasingly post-Christian era. Even dark clouds have silver linings.

In this chapter I propose several elements of what I believe is a Christ-centered political engagement. Despite inevitable disagreements over electoral outcomes and preferred policies, Christians from across the political divide should embrace a distinctly Christian posture in our politics, one that distinguishes us from the rest of the world. This means speaking consistently and, when needed, prophetically. It means being humble yet strong and doing politics for justice, not merely winning. Ultimately, it means keeping our eyes where they belong—on Jesus's empty tomb and the hope it provides—while rejecting false promises of temporal political wins in the process.

Christians can seek political victories in pursuit of justice for our communities and neighbors. Political power is not inherently suspect; well-ordered politics is an essential element of our kingdom witness to the world. But I am convinced that *how* we seek and wield this power matters. In John 17, Jesus prays that while his disciples "are not of the world," he has nevertheless "sent them into the world" and asks God for their sanctification.[3] With this in mind, the motives and motivations driving our political decision making are just as important as outcomes. As Christians, they *must* be.

This, I believe, is the beginning of a better political engagement.

---

3. John 17:14–18.

A Better Political Engagement

WHAT IS "POLITICAL ENGAGEMENT"?

First, a word on political engagement. This is a term frequently thrown around by Christian writers and thinkers, often alluding to different things. For one person, political engagement might mean pursuing a career in government or public policy. For another, it could mean speaking out on political, social, and cultural issues in one's community, leaning firmly on her Christian worldview. For another, it may be educating oneself on salient issues and becoming more aware of what is happening in national, state, and local politics. And for another, it might be as simple as determining how to vote in each election.

By "political engagement" I am referring to how people interact with the political environment around them. Mine is a broad, holistic understanding, encompassing the smallest (e.g., voting) and largest (e.g., careers) of actions. Some engagement may be more active, involving efforts to shape or transform some element of the political system. Some engagement may be more passive, involving endeavors aimed more at personal enrichment and education. But at the heart of political engagement is an intentional effort to approach and make sense of the world around us. Political engagement can take many forms. What is critical is the intention to reach out to the political world and consider how this world will shape you.

I tell new and prospective students that studying political science does not necessarily forebode a career in government, policy, or electoral politics. Yes, some of our graduates do this, most recently with interest groups and elected officials. But most of our political science alums go into work and life with (at best) a tangential connection to the traditional political process. Studying politics and political science is more than just following election returns and keeping up with the latest developments in Washington, DC. It involves reading carefully, writing precisely, and thinking critically—and at Christian universities such as mine, it involves considering how faith shapes and guides our perceptions of the political world. A better political engagement should aim for these habits and the following principles.

Be Consistent and Prophetic

A Christian political engagement ought to be both consistent and prophetic. Consistent political engagement means not adjusting one's views to fit changing narratives or circumstances. It means saying the same things in the same ways regardless of political context. It means praising and critiquing political actors and parties when warranted without regard to their identity. It means your deepest convictions drive your political viewpoints, not the other way around.

Similarly, prophetic political engagement means being willing to say unpopular things in your community, especially when it puts you at odds with shifting political conventions. It emphasizes steadily speaking the truth regardless of what it means for your standing in your political tribe. It means holding your community to account free from the temptations that come with negative partisanship. Together, a consistent and prophetic political engagement looks very different from the world's brand of politics.

Consistency is often lacking in politics, particularly at an elite level. Leading up to the 2016 election, Donald Trump and other Republicans routinely criticized government unemployment numbers as incomplete or outright biased in favor of Democrats.[4] "They say 5.3 percent unemployment," Trump said in October 2015. "The number is probably 32 percent." Trump routinely called these figures "phony" and at one point called them "one of the biggest hoaxes in modern politics." But in March 2017, Trump's press secretary Sean Spicer went to the White House podium to tout declining unemployment numbers, saying, "I talked to the president prior to this, and he said to quote him very clearly: 'They may have been phony in the past, but it's very real now.'"[5]

One of my favorite examples of inconsistency in political decision making and arguments has to do with something called the debt ceiling. If you didn't know, the United States government borrows a lot of money to pay for its programs (as I'm writing this, the national debt stands at just over $31 trillion). Economists are generally comfortable with this method of deficit spending since the American economy is large enough to account for our growing debt without putting the country at serious risk of not being able to pay this money back to our debt holders. To draw on the wisdom of Hall of Fame basketball player Patrick Ewing, the US government spends a lot of money, but its economy generates a lot of money.[6]

---

4. Ingraham, "19 Times Trump Called Jobs Numbers 'Fake.'"

5. Conway, "Spicer Claims That Jobs Numbers 'May Have Been Phony.'"

6. During the 1999 National Basketball Association labor crisis, Ewing tried to rally support for the players by explaining that professional athletes "make a lot of money, but spend a lot of money." Not surprisingly, that argument did not play especially well with the public. See Beck, "Public Relations a Concern."

A Better Political Engagement

To continue borrowing money, Congress must occasionally pass what amounts to an increase on the country's credit card limit. This is because there is a legal limit on how much the government can borrow, and adjusting this limit requires action from Congress. To add another wrinkle, the government often has already spent or agreed to spend money in upcoming bills that it legally can't spend without raising the debt ceiling. So, the debt ceiling does not exclusively bind future spending but also past spending. If this ceiling is not raised, the government cannot borrow funds to pay its lenders what they are owed. And virtually all economists agree that this would trigger a global economic meltdown.[7]

As you can see, the whole process is a bit of a mess. And elite elected officials have taken advantage of this process to demonstrate some brazen inconsistencies in how they approach this issue. When Barack Obama was president, a faction of Republicans demanded concessions (including spending cuts) in exchange for their votes to raise the debt ceiling, while Democrats (including President Obama) argued that raising the debt ceiling should be "clean"—that is, independent of other considerations. This disagreement almost led to an unprecedented government default, and various financial agencies temporarily downgraded the United States' credit rating.[8]

However, when Donald Trump was president, the tenor of Republican and Democratic arguments changed. To be sure, there was a contingent of Republicans who argued for spending cuts in exchange for raising the debt ceiling, but Republican leadership was not swayed by these demands in supporting Trump's efforts to lift the ceiling. Democrats, on the other hand, used this instance to extract concessions of their own—specifically, raising federal spending by $50 billion for the following fiscal year.[9] Partisan flips on the debt ceiling and other issues—including confirming judges, the legislative filibuster, and keeping the government fully funded—are textbook examples of inconsistencies in American politics.

Earlier, I highlighted research showing how the average American is not particularly sophisticated in their political ideology, meaning our political beliefs are not deeply rooted. When so many of our political opinions and ideas are top-down, driven by elites through cooperative media, we can find ourselves behaving inconsistently without much effort. A great example

---

7. Sheiner and Sheiner, "How Worried Should We Be If the Debt Ceiling Isn't Lifted?"
8. Balkin, "Not-So-Happy Anniversary of the Debt-Ceiling Crisis."
9. Mui, Pramuk, and Mitra, "White House, Congress Strike."

of this is in public opinion on the economy. According to Gallup, "Republicans' and Democrats' views of the economy have consistently differed over the years, depending on which party controls the White House."[10] Indeed, these opinions shift quickly—immediately following the 2016 presidential election, Democrats' views on the health of the economy fell by 37 percentage points, while Republicans' rose by 80 percent. No economic conditions had changed; only the person in the White House had.

Consistency must be part of a robust Christian political engagement. Consider Jesus's words in the Sermon on the Mount, where he tells the crowd, "Let what you say be simply 'Yes' or 'No.'"[11] Jesus said this about swearing oaths in God's name, but it isn't hard to see how this principle also applies to consistent behavior and principles. Christians should let our political yeses be yeses and our nos be nos, regardless of consequences; consistency goes hand in hand with honesty, among others and ourselves. Moreover, in the Old Testament it is written that authorities were looking for excuses to arrest Daniel, the Jewish adviser to the Babylonian king. "But they could find no ground for complaint or any fault," it is written, "because he was faithful, and no error or fault was found in him."[12] It could be said that Daniel lived his life, in the private and public squares, with consistency—he was who he appeared to be.

I am increasingly convinced that a consistent political engagement will eventually be prophetic, largely because of the impermanent dynamics of politics and political action. Consider the Republican Party's changing position on free trade to align with Donald Trump's message of economic populism and protectionism or the Democratic Party's changing position on civil rights in the 1950s and sixties. While seemingly intractable in the moment, the values and goals of the nation's major political parties *do* change over time. As a result, a consistent political engagement will inevitably cause a steadfast member of a political party to one day be on the outside looking in, heralding a now-unpopular opinion to a skeptical and critical audience. And while our beliefs certainly can change with new information and evidence, we must be careful that they are not changing just because the political environment demands it.

What does a prophetic political engagement look like? Consider two former members of Congress from Michigan: Bart Stupak and Peter Meijer.

---

10. McCarthy, "2017 Partisan Gap in Economic Confidence One of the Largest."
11. Matthew 5:37.
12. Daniel 6:4.

Stupak, a Christian, was first elected as a pro-life Democrat in 1992 but came to national prominence during wrangling over the health care reform debates of President Obama's first term. Stupak supported the legislation but also wanted to prevent the bill from publicly funding abortions. Those on the left attacked him for seeking to limit abortion funding, while those on the right attacked him for supporting the work of a Democratic president. Following Obama's promise to issue an executive order barring abortion funding in the bill and facing challenges from pro-choice and pro-life groups, Stupak announced he would not run for reelection. Though once at home in the Democratic Party, Stupak and other pro-life Democrats found out what a consistent political engagement might bring: political exile.[13]

Peter Meijer's story is different from Stupak's, yet still similar. Elected as a Republican in 2020, one of Meijer's first votes as a congressman was in the impeachment trial of President Trump. Meijer's belief that Trump's actions on January 6 violated his oath of office led him to vote to impeach the president, making him one of a handful of Republican congressmen to do so. He called voting to impeach Trump "career suicide before my career even began."[14] Meijer's decision was not popular in the moment, nor did it lead to career advancement in Republican Party politics: he was defeated for reelection by a primary challenger in 2022.[15] Still, this did not keep Meijer from speaking and acting prophetically when he was convinced it was desperately needed. "I would rather lose office with my character intact," he later said, "than stay reelected having made sacrifices of the soul."[16]

Or consider the voices of Justin Giboney and David French. Giboney became politically active with the Democratic Party in Atlanta, serving as a delegate for the party's 2012 national convention. And while most of Giboney's political views align with his party, his pro-life views make him an outsider to more influential Democrats.[17] French, meanwhile, has become one of the conservative movement's leading "Never Trump" voices.[18] French consistently—and, after Trump won his party's nomination for the

---

13. Cai, "Anti-Abortion Democrats Are a Dying Breed."

14. Alberta, "What the GOP Does to Its Own Dissenters."

15. Meijer's defeat was aided with funding from the Democratic Party, which believed it would be easier to win a general election against someone other than Meijer. See Weigel, Itkowitz, and Singh, "GOP's Meijer Voted to Impeach Trump"

16. Berg, "Meijer."

17. Giboney, Wear, and Butler, *Compassion (&) Conviction.*

18. Ross, "Who, Exactly, Is David French, the 'Never Trump' White Knight Candidate?"

presidency, prophetically—wrote and spoke against Trump as a candidate and president, even when he agreed with some aspects of his presidency.[19] These views gained him some influence on the right but netted him far more opponents. Both Giboney and French, like Stupak and Meijer, have been consistent (and eventually prophetic) in their political engagement, despite the consequences that followed.

To be clear, a prophetic political engagement does not mean we should not speak out against actors or views emanating from "the other side" or that we should train our political fire solely on our communities. Our Christian convictions must always drive our political engagement, regardless of audience. Just as we should not minimize conflict in our communities by ignoring or glossing over the logs in our own eye, we should not seek to minimize conflicts with the world in the name of promoting temporary harmony. Our approach ought to balance truth *and* grace, not one or the other. We cannot play favorites in our political responsibilities.

Still, there is a real temptation to focus the bulk of our attention on our opponents while leaving our allies relatively unscathed. After all, the thinking goes, *they're* the real problem, *they're* the graver threat, and any issues in *our* group pale in comparison. The problem with this thinking is its tendency to warp not only our behavior but also our deeper convictions. Consider a survey question from the Public Religion Research Institute asking, "Do you think an elected official who commits an immoral act in their private life can still behave ethically and fulfill their duties in their public and professional life?"[20] In 2011, just 30 percent of white evangelicals said this would be possible. But during the 2016 presidential campaign, with Donald Trump on the ballot, that number ballooned to 72 percent, by far the highest change among any religious group.

Consistency is not easy. It requires humility (more on that in a moment). It requires thoughtfulness. It requires boldness. And it requires the belief that your actions, however miniscule and fleeting they may seem, matter a great deal as a living testament of the gospel to a lost and fallen world. This is true whether you identify as a strong Republican, a steadfast Democrat, a hopeful third party member, or are wandering in the political wilderness. In our imperfect world with imperfect choices, we all must take positions that will sometimes test our commitment to consistency and open us up to criticism from multiple flanks.

19. French, "Complete Case for Kavanaugh."
20. Galston, "Has Trump Caused White Evangelicals to Change Their Tune on Morality?"

But consistency does not impede effective political engagement; it is a prerequisite to an authentic and faithful engagement, one formed by a Christian worldview, not warping it. A consistent and prophetic approach to politics is required for Christians to take seriously our identity of being "in the world, not of the world." Consistency may make short-term political action more difficult or uncomfortable, but it is essential for a long-term kingdom vision of political engagement. No, consistency is not easy. But the right thing often isn't.

Be Humble Yet Strong

As a child, I was taught that Jesus was a meek leader whose interactions with authorities on behalf of his ministry and the oppressed confounded the status quo. He led with love, not with force. He was, to borrow language from one Christmas carol, tender and mild. He was not, as many Jews of the day were hoping, a revolutionary political leader; to their chagrin, his kingdom would not be of this world. And sure, at times he showed anger, primarily directed at religious leaders of the day and toward those corrupting sacred spaces in Jerusalem. But these examples were rare and only served to reinforce that Jesus tended toward gentleness and lowliness.

It wasn't until I was older that I recognized that this depiction of Jesus as tender and mild was incomplete. Jesus was not a stoic and disconnected leader, walking through life in a holy daze. He prayed fervently. He expressed anger. He wept for his friends. He was discouraged by the faithlessness of his closest disciples. Jesus was God, of course, but he was also a man—a perfect man, tempted though uncorrupted by sin, but a man all the same. It can be difficult to balance these conceptions of Jesus: The loving and tender teacher, and the passionate and confident leader. Our fallen minds struggle to see him for who he really is.

We encounter this difficulty all the time today. As American evangelicalism has tended to emphasize the loving tenderness of Jesus in our efforts to reach others with the good news of the gospel, this has sometimes shaped our behaviors toward the world. Some have made sure not to react to sin with harshness but with love and grace. There is an emphasis on making peace with the world for the sake of maintaining a public witness; too harsh a rebuke, the thinking may go, will close doors for future evangelism. Others, seeing a decline in culture and a rise in ideologies inconsistent with a traditional Christian ethic, react more forcefully to these things without regard to the "feelings" of the world. Christ is King, they may say, and God will not be mocked.

This latter approach has seen increased attention following the presidencies of Donald Trump and Joe Biden. In his essay for *First Things*, Aaron Renn proposed a new framework for thinking through Christian political engagement.[21] He broke down the history of Christian engagement in America into "three worlds," or eras, each world requiring something different from Christians in engaging the world around us. In the early, *positive* world, Renn described a world in which Christianity was largely seen as a positive good for American society. In this context, Christians could approach politics and culture without much difficulty, for the rest of society, even if not explicitly Christian, still saw the value of Christian influence in America as an integral part of the culture's civil religion.

The 1990s brought us into a second world, which Renn called the *neutral* world. Here, Christianity was no longer necessary for sociocultural and political flourishing. Pluralism and increasing rates of secularism showed a way forward for society beyond the traditional Christian worldview. Though Christianity remained a valid option among many, it became just another belief system. The Supreme Court's decision in *Obergefell v. Hodges* ushered in the third and current world, the *negative* world. In the negative world, Renn wrote, "Christian morality is expressly repudiated and seen as a threat to the public good and the new public moral order. Subscribing to Christian moral views or violating the secular moral order brings negative consequences."

According to Renn, this framework has immense consequences for Christian political engagement. The engagement strategies in the positive world—and, to an extent, the neutral world—no longer make sense in a culture hostile to Christianity. Moreover, those wedded to older models of engagement may find themselves tempted to capitulate to changing cultural norms and mores in the name of maintaining relationships. This is, according to Renn, especially true for elite-adjacent evangelicals, who occupy positions of cultural influence and now find themselves with a great deal to lose. Indeed, Renn believes such a transformation has already begun. "Under pressure, this group has turned away from engagement with and toward synchronization with secular elite culture, particularly around matters such as race and immigration," he writes. "Their rhetoric in these areas is increasingly strident and ever more aligned with secular political

---

21. Renn, "Three Worlds of Evangelicalism."

positions." This group contrasts with blue-collar and rural evangelicals, who never had this kind of elite access in the first place.

Theologian James Wood has also written about necessary changes to Christian political engagement. In a *First Things* essay of his own, Wood explained how he "evolved" on Tim Keller and his approach to engaging politics.[22] Specifically, Wood critiqued *winsomeness*[23] in Christian political engagement, something embodied in Keller's post-partisan, third-way politics.[24] "An excessive concern to appeal to the unchurched," Wood wrote, "is plagued by the accommodationist temptation. This is all the more a problem in the 'negative world.'" Wood also critiqued a reliance on winsomeness meant to preserve social standing and relationships, especially among Christians in elite-adjacent spaces like journalism and academia. Winsomeness, understood in this way, could become just as much of an idol as raw political power.

Wood's essay attracted a lot of attention, including from David French. He said that Wood's argument implies that political ends justify any means, especially those that require rejecting a winsome approach to political engagement in pursuit of political victories.[25] Other critics, like pastor Derek Radney, argued that winsomeness is not a political strategy but rather a genuine approach to engaging the world across myriad venues—not to maintain the status quo for self-interested actors, but to demonstrate God's patience and love to a world in need, regardless of how such an approach is received.[26] In response, Wood clarified and reiterated his perspective that the focus on a winsome public witness "leads Christians, often and in various ways, to let the broader culture set the terms for our engagement out of fear about negative perception."[27]

Wood expanded on his critique of winsomeness in a talk at the 2022 National Conservatism Conference, which was later summarized in an essay for *The American Conservative*. For Wood, being winsome means downplaying divisions and deprioritizing political victories. "Winsomeness makes us think about politics through the lens of evangelism," he wrote. "Thus, our political judgments and actions are filtered through

22. Wood, "How I Evolved on Tim Keller."
23. "Winsomeness" is defined as pleasing, charming, and appealing in demeanor.
24. James, "Is It Time to Move Past Tim Keller?"
25. French, "Critique of Tim Keller Reveals the Moral Devolution."
26. Radney, "Here Is Where James & Rennites Miss Keller."
27. Wood, "This Article Is Not About Tim Keller."

how likely they will make our neighbors to receive the gospel message."[28] A better approach for Christians, Wood thinks, involves focusing less on how the world sees us and more on advocating policies and political action consistent with the Christian tradition. "Focus on seeking justice, speak the truth, and stand firm," he concludes. "Don't let an obsession with appearing winsome hinder us from a robust pursuit of winning some of our cultural battles for the common good."

While writers like Renn and Wood raise important points about the changing realities confronting Christians today, some of their assumptions and resulting solutions are questionable. For example, Renn assumes that life for Christians after *Obergefell* is demonstrably worse than in previous eras, but this is, at best, speculative. In response to Renn and others, French cites his experience as a religious liberty attorney and the hostility government has expressed toward Christian communities for decades. That, coupled with increased constitutional protections for the free exercise of religion and speech won by Christian political and legal advocacy, paints a decidedly different picture of American society than Renn's negative world framing.[29] Things *are* challenging for Christians today, as I wrote just a chapter ago. But this does not necessarily demand a completely different engagement strategy than those from past eras.

Yet this is the crux of Wood's argument about winsomeness as a stumbling block to effective political engagement. Winsomeness, he argues, erroneously conflates evangelism with political action: "Politics is not about maximizing openness to the gospel message. Rather, politics is about ordering our common life together. It is the prudential pursuit of justice and a just social order." By incorrectly grouping evangelism (and apologetics) with political engagement, Christians artificially limit their political effectiveness. Therefore, for Wood, Christians must be willing to abandon winsomeness if it leads to greater opportunities for political victories, especially victories that advance the common good.

Toward the end of his essay on winsomeness, Wood summarizes his approach:

> Certainly, we must be willing to lose, and we must not lose our souls in the pursuit of winning. But we must intend to win in the political realm as we seek to promote the good, protect the weak, and love our neighbors. *We must ignore the accusations that cripple*

---

28. Wood, "Limits of Winsome Politics."
29. French, "Critique of Tim Keller Reveals the Moral Devolution."

A Better Political Engagement

those who, appropriating the winsome approach, are too concerned about how Christians are viewed by others [emphasis added].

Wood and I agree on the need to lose well despite our best efforts and on the importance of using political power for the sake of justice and neighbor.[30] But it is a mistake to think that Christians emphasizing winsomeness do so solely to minimize conflict with the world or to maintain some status with secular elites. Wood seems to have a negative view of winsomeness, equating it with political naivete or unfamiliarity with the seriousness that our current moment demands. But this is just one understanding of winsomeness as it pertains to political engagement.

What if Christians prioritize winsomeness not out of weakness but out of confidence? What if a winsome political engagement is a genuine and strategic effort to shape political outcomes? While some might lean on winsomeness out of fear of offending or mitigating conflict, others might do so because they genuinely believe it is a biblical and consistent approach to successful political engagement. Consider how Christian colleges and universities in California reacted to a bill that would have restricted where students could use state grant funding. These colleges lobbied vigorously against the bill, to be sure, but they did so in a decidedly winsome way, meeting with state representatives and senators who had otherwise had no contact with those in Christian higher education. The result was a compromise measure that appeared to change the minds of elected officials regarding the purpose and motives of Christian higher education.[31]

What does all this have to do with humility and strength in our political engagement as Christians? Quite a lot. In addition to a consistent and prophetic voice, Christians should be humble enough not to transform our witness to the world—including our political engagement—based on the world's changing circumstances. Yes, we should adapt to changing circumstances in the ways in which we faithfully engage, but this does not mean we should change what faithful engagement looks like in the first place. For example, in an environment where *Roe v. Wade* no longer governs abortion policy in the United States, Christians' activism against abortion should not look the same as it did from 1973 to 2022. But if biblical winsomeness was good for a particular era, it is also good for this one. Our political environment may change, but this should not affect on our political posture. We should be humble enough to resist the temptation of overcorrection.

---

30. Bennett, "We Need to Be Better Losers."
31. Mendoza, "How a California Bill Became a Lesson in Compromise."

Humility of this sort should be grounded in at least two principles. First, humility should trust that our efforts will not be in vain, even if these efforts don't yield the political and cultural outcomes we had hoped for (I'll return to this shortly). Political engagement matters not merely because of the victories we achieve but also because of how it is an outgrowth of our faith and identity in Christ. We should seek the flourishing of our neighbors and communities through the political process, and this flourishing is best found in the Christian tradition. But this does not mean we should abandon our constitutional structure or ditch established political norms to achieve it. For Christians, pluralism under republican democracy means vigorously contesting elections and engaging the policy process while at the same time recognizing that results are not everything.

Second, humility should acknowledge that what we think is *a* right outcome may not be *the* right outcome. In his excellent book *How the Nations Rage*, Jonathan Leeman distinguishes between straight- and jagged-line issues. The Bible speaks clearly on straight-line issues (e.g., abortion) but not on jagged-line issues (e.g., marginal tax rates). "So much political dialogue among Christians these days," Leeman writes, "thoughtlessly and divisively treats everything as a straight-line issue."[32] And I'll go a step further: solutions to straight-line issues do not require straight-line answers. Christians can—and should—agree that abortion is a moral calamity, but this doesn't require Christians to agree on policy solutions to abortion, especially when neither major political party offers comprehensive solutions to this problem. We can disagree on the complexities of the political process without casting aspersions on the legitimacy of another's faith.

At the same time, strength is essential for a better Christian political engagement. James Wood concludes his essay critiquing winsomeness by emphasizing the need to stand firm in the face of an increasingly hostile culture. He is right to say this—on issues and ideas central to our faith, Christians must not cede ground to maintain peace with the world. But strength should not be confused with machismo or adopting the strategies of our non-Christian culture, even when these strategies may seem to be more effective at the moment. In Gethsemane, Peter thought strength meant drawing the sword; Jesus's strength was something else entirely.

Our political engagement as Christians is not the same as Jesus preparing to go to the cross. But his example and instruction throughout Scripture—immediately before his crucifixion and elsewhere—are valuable

---

32. Leeman, *How the Nations Rage*, 93.

all the same. Jesus's call for his followers to "turn the other cheek" is often cited as a reason for passiveness, or even pacifism, among Christians. But a better reading of this passage indicates yet another way Christians are to be not of this world in how we interact with our fellow image bearers. The world's response to injustice or threats is to strike back in kind, while the Christian's response confounds the status quo with real, authentic strength.

Politics gives us some of the highest stakes imaginable. It affects us, our families, our neighbors, our communities, and our world. Elections have consequences that can last for decades, even generations. Given these high stakes, it is understandable why so many people view political battles with great urgency. How many times have you heard that *this* election is the most important of your lifetime? Yes, they say it every year, but *this* year it's true, isn't it? So it isn't surprising when this urgency provokes worldly strength to meet worldly challenges. As it is in Renn's account of the negative world, the urgency of our moment demands an equivalently strong political response.

But it takes a different kind of strength entirely to approach this urgency with the patience and faith that Jesus wants for us. It was only when Peter looked away from Jesus that he began to sink into the sea. In that moment he doubted Jesus's perfect strength and instead relied on his own senses, his understanding of what was required. Likewise, the Jewish people had been waiting centuries for their promised Messiah, who would usher in a new order and cast off their oppressors. But they were so certain of who they expected that they missed the deliverer in their midst. Though the stakes in our politics may seem impossibly high, Christian political engagement must be first and foremost *Christian*. We must hold our citizenship and our politics less tightly than our hope and confidence in our risen savior.

This does not mean our political engagement should lack strength or passion. Jesus gave plenty of examples of righteous anger and forceful responses. But for us, as fallen people, picking our moments is vital. We should treat politics with the seriousness it deserves while refusing to join in the daily melees that too often dominate our political discourse. With a wealth of information and news at our fingertips, this is a seductive temptation. In her book *Untrustworthy*, Bonnie Kristian writes, "If you follow more stories than you can follow well, you're not better-informed. You're distracted."[33] Our real strength—and the patience, love, and wisdom that come with it—is found not in social media platforms or political activism

---

33. Kristian, *Untrustworthy*, 182.

but in nothing less than Jesus himself. "If you're outraged at everything, you're not like Jesus," wrote *The Gospel Coalition*'s Matt Smethurst, before continuing, "If you're outraged at nothing, you're not like Jesus."[34]

Some Christians have criticized prominent Christian voices like Tim Keller and Russell Moore for a supposed tendency toward appeasing hostile cultural forces through tone and posture. There may have been a moment for this kind of political engagement, it is said, but given the distinct challenges of our post-Christian society, that moment has passed. David French offers a gentle corrective, writing, "When fear and hatred dominates discourse, a commitment to justice *and* kindness *and* humility is precisely what the moment requires."[35] And Paul, writing to the church in Colossae, instructs, "Walk in wisdom toward outsiders, making the best use of the time. Let your speech always be gracious, seasoned with salt, so that you may know how you ought to answer each person."[36] A commitment to humility and biblical strength does not mean backing away from the political fray. Rather, it acknowledges that how we do politics matters just as much as what we gain from it.

Seek Justice, Not Victories

Political conflicts are often seen as *zero-sum games*. In economics, a zero-sum game is a contest between at least two parties where one party winning means the others lose.[37] It is easy for us to understand politics in this way, especially in our system with two major parties and a winner-take-all system of voting and elections. Consider an election where, say, five million people vote: so long as Candidate A gets one more vote than Candidate B, Candidate A wins 100 percent of that election. In a lot of ways, our electoral system is the essence of a zero-sum game. The winner gets everything, and the loser gets nothing.

In practice, though, our policy and political conflicts are far from zero-sum. The American political process is designed to encourage—to require, really—compromise, so any outcome to a conflict rarely gives one party everything it wants. Writing in *Federalist 10*, James Madison believed

34. Smethurst, "If You're Outraged at Everything, You're Not like Jesus."
35. French, "Critique of Tim Keller Reveals the Moral Devolution."
36. Colossians 4:5–6
37. A coin toss or game of rock-paper-scissors are simple examples of zero-sum games—in each, there is a winner and a loser, and nothing in between.

that it is only by encouraging the proliferation of factions can the American political experiment escape the tyranny of the majority, wherein one group or perspective dominates the others all the time. Crucially, an increased number of factions in our midst requires more and more compromise and cooperation among these factions for effective governance. In today's most heated and difficult policy debates, what ends up passing Congress rarely satisfies anybody completely—and if you're a passionate partisan, you may regularly feel like the other side is getting all the breaks.

That said, compromise for the sake of compromise is not the goal. Faithful political engagement does not mean dispassionately surrendering important terrain to those who disagree with us just for the sake of "niceness." Instead, our political engagement as Christians means wading into our political system to seek justice for our communities rather than simply beating our opponents. And while seeking justice often requires winning elections, our motives as Christians must matter. Given the allure of negative partisanship and the apocalyptic tenor so often consuming our political debates, it can be easy to adopt the world's win-at-all-costs mentality. But Christians are not of the world. We can reject this mentality with confidence and faith, focusing instead on a holistic pursuit of justice free from the constraints of specific elections and limits of imperfect candidates.

Not considering winning an essential goal can draw its share of critics. William Wolfe is one of them. "Here's one of the biggest problems with conservatives in America," he wrote in October 2022. "They would rather lose nobly, even to wicked [and] evil enemies, than win in an ugly manner. They want to feel good about themselves, though they let their country be overrun by tyrants, [than] do what it takes to win."[38] A common refrain during the Trump era was "But he fights!," the implication being that while Trump may be a transgressive political figure, his results speak for themselves.[39] Likewise, Rod Dreher has written admirably of Hungary's Viktor Orban and his heavy-handedness when dealing with his political opponents.[40] For these voices, seeking justice and securing victories go hand in hand, since Christians can only achieve the justice we seek by winning political battles.

The danger of this perspective is that it risks elevating political victories to the same level as pursuing justice, equating the means with the ends and confusing their order. What happens when we view political outcomes

---

38. Wolfe, "Here's One of the Biggest Problems with Conservatives in America."
39. Sayet, "He May Be Crass, but This Man Fights."
40. Wallace-Wells, "What American Conservatives See in Hungary's Leader."

with primacy? We tend to make concessions to convictions that should be more deeply rooted. Author Samuel James believes the temptation of political power—whether out of fear or lust—has corrupted some evangelicals' understanding of the right order between politics, ethics, and theology. "The political tail," he said on an episode of the "Upstream" podcast, "is wagging the theological dog."[41] My pastor, Ted Wenger, described this relationship well in a March 2022 sermon: "We are to love God and use the world, not the other way around."

Scripture is replete with commands to seek the good of our neighbors, communities, and world as a matter of first principle. In Jeremiah's account of Israel in exile, God instructs the people not only to submit to their rulers (foreshadowing Romans 13 and 1 Peter 2), but to seek and pray for the good of their communities. "But seek the welfare of the city where I have sent you into exile," Jeremiah recounts, "and pray to the Lord on its behalf, for in its welfare you will find your welfare."[42] It can be tempting for Christians today to look at our surroundings and resulting challenges and decide to bide our time, waiting for political changes or transformations better suited to our interests and ends. But this is not scriptural; we are to not only pray for our cities, states, and nation, but to actively seek the good of these communities and institutions.

Similarly, the prophet Micah provides perhaps the most well-known synopsis of this charge to God's people. "He has told you, O man, what is good," the prophet writes, "and what does the Lord require of you but to do justice, and to love kindness, and to walk humbly with your God?"[43] These three things—doing justice, loving kindness, and walking humbly—ought to be at the center of any Christian political engagement. We must seek to do justice in kindness and humility. This does not mean watering down biblical justice to preserve our secular status. But it does mean we should be able to do justice and seek the well-being of our neighbors with a kindness that confounds and puzzles the world and with humility that demonstrates our deeper confidence in the truth. Being strong in our convictions does not mean being jerks.

What does it mean to prioritize justice over victories, especially in the context of commands to obey and respect our governing authorities? First, it means routinely checking our attitudes and motivations for political

---

41. Morris, "Politics and Prophetic Witness." See the ten minute mark.
42. Jeremiah 29:7.
43. Micah 6:8.

engagement. Ask yourself: Why do I care so much about this election or this legislative battle? Is it because of an earnest desire to see good advanced in the world, or is it because, deep down, I get joy from seeing my opponents defeated? The latter may be a necessary outcome in the pursuit of justice in our midst, but it is by no means sufficient. Christians should unequivocally reject the temporary allure of negative partisanship, and instead focus on a deeper and richer substance in our political engagement.

I am not saying Christians must adopt a "too liberal for Republicans, too conservative for Democrats" ethos in crafting a better political engagement. Critiquing America's major political parties by refusing to side with either—often called "third way-ism"—has its merits, but also its challenges. On the merits, Tim Keller has clearly called for Christians to approach politics in this way, including in one *New York Times* essay titled, "How Do Christians Fit into the Two-Party System? They Don't."[44] Tyler Huckabee, on the other hand, referred to third way-ism as a "nebulous target," tempting Christians to dismiss real political challenges at times when there are important differences between Republicans and Democrats. Christians may opt for this sort of centrism, Huckabee said, because it *feels* like an enlightened alternative to partisanship, when in reality it is simply equivocation.[45]

Refusing to align with both Democrats and Republicans is a reasonable tack to take, but it is not required to do politics well. A Christian can be a committed and convicted partisan who nevertheless keeps politics in its right place, subordinate to her identity in Christ. At the same time, a Christian can reject partisanship as a flawed dichotomy while nevertheless rejecting the sort of posture I propose here. What matters is not our *political* identity; what matters is how we *understand* this identity considering our hope in Christ. A consistent, humble, strong, and justice-seeking posture can be found among political conservatives and liberals—and the politically homeless—in the body of Christ. Third way-ism, though a valid approach to our political conflicts, is not the outcome of a better political engagement.

Second, it means being creative in our political engagement and advocacy but not obstinate in our defeats. There must be a middle ground between a political nihilism that rejects engagement as a fruitless endeavor and a political apocalypticism that considers our efforts to be the last stand against impending doom. Christians must accept political setbacks and

---

44. Keller, "How Do Christians Fit Into the Two-Party System?"
45. Huckabee, "Sunday's Cool."

electoral defeats as temporary (and at times inevitable) losses in a pluralist system, not existential threats. There will always be another election, another opportunity to seek the good of our neighbors. As I will argue in the next chapter, we cannot throw out the rule book when results don't go our way. America's political framework has served its people well; a negative outcome or two does not necessitate abandoning this system altogether.

Speaking on the same episode of the "Upstream" podcast, Samuel James warned against the temptation of adopting the political strategies of the world solely because of their perceived effectiveness in achieving our goals:

> We've fallen for a kind of sociopolitical prosperity gospel when we expect faithfulness to Jesus to result in cultural victories, in political influence, and in personal enrichment for ourselves and our institutions. We have to embrace the fact that we do not have the freedom to use the tools of culture war that secular culture actually uses. We have to embrace the fact that our savior was nailed to a cross and let it happen.[46]

Our political engagement should serve the common good and promote justice in our midst, not simply defeat our opponents or make our lives as comfortable as possible. And while there will be divisions among Christians about what precisely this requires in terms of government action (or inaction), we can hopefully agree on the right ends while continuing to debate and contest the means of getting there. This is where Christians can stand in sharp contrast to the world. We should, as my former youth pastor would say, remember to keep the main thing the main thing.

Elections have consequences. Christians supporting, say, restrictions on abortion and protections for religious freedom must consider the 2016 presidential election one of the most consequential in recent history, with the three Supreme Court nominations President Trump was able to make during his four years in office. But elections must not be the determinant of our confidence and security. Regardless of how our elections turn out, we should instead confess the words of that timeless hymn that our hope is built on nothing less than Jesus's blood and righteousness. We should vote. We should work to elect candidates that share the values we hold. But we should not compromise these values in the name of temporal victories or inconsistently apply political ethics on a case-by-case or

---

46. Morris, "Politics and Prophetic Witness." See the thirty-three minute mark.

candidate-by-candidate basis. We must not equivocate or rationalize. Our battle has already been won.

Keep Your Eyes on the Cross

According to *Christianity Today*, Matthew Pierce is "the undisputed king of weird evangelical Twitter."[47] He is also the author of the satirical *Evangelical Thought Leader: The Liturgy of Radically Engaging the Culture of Paradigm Shifts*.[48] The book's chapters include subjects like worship music, marriage, theology, and yes, politics. At one point in his chapter on the latter, Pierce, perfectly in character, writes

> Some Christians will say that it's not the Church's job to get political, that we must lead with the Gospel or something. With charity in my heart, I must say to those morons: you are totally wrong. We would do well to remember Jesus' words "render unto Caesar," which was about taxation without representation. The point is, Jesus was getting political, and if Jesus did something that was easy to do, then I will, too.[49]

Pierce's writing is a parody, but it is such a hit because it is so close to the truth. Christians can easily flock to one of two extremes when it comes to engaging politics. We may approach politics in a way very much of the world, our behaviors indiscernible from our non-Christian neighbors. Conversely, we may reject the apparent filthiness of politics and believe the best Christian kind of political engagement is a rejection of politics entirely.

Neither of these approaches are ideal. Christians cannot ignore politics to supposedly keep our hands clean from the grime of the political world. Political engagement is a certainty of living in community; ignoring politics doesn't change this. At the same time, our posture and approach to politics must be confounding to the world's understanding of politics. Consistency, humility, and an orientation to justice should dominate Christian political engagement rather than toxic partisanship, bravado, and a strategy emphasizing winning at any and all costs. We must be honest in assessing the strengths and weaknesses of Democrats and Republicans as our two

---

47. Silliman, "Knock Knock."
48. Pierce, *Evangelical Thought Leader*.
49. Pierce, *Evangelical Thought Leader*, 69.

major political choices.[50] We can be faithful in our partisanship and faithful in our nonpartisanship.

I have memories from my childhood of my mother referencing a southern gospel song titled "This World is Not My Home."[51] I don't recall singing the song at church, but I remember the lyrics and tune well. The song begins with a short verse:

> This world is not my home, I'm just a-passing through;
> My treasures are laid up somewhere beyond the blue;
> The angels beckon me from heaven's open door,
> And I can't feel at home in this world any more.

I wouldn't characterize this verse as promoting an ascetic or disconnected Christianity, one that encourages an aloofness from the troubles and trials of the world. Instead, it is a healthy reminder of the limits of politics to truly save us. Yes, politics and elections matter. It matters who governs us and how. But ultimately, what Tim Keller said at the beginning of this chapter is correct: when we think politics can save or redeem us and our communities, it becomes a dangerous and corrupting idol. As Christians, it is always important to remember that while we must not neglect our attention to and work in the world, it is ultimately not our home. Our eyes must be affixed most securely not to polls, campaigns, or court cases, but to the cross.

There is no shortage of challenges for Christians in our political and cultural engagement in the years ahead. Here, I hope to have shown the importance of a consistent, humble, and justice-oriented political posture. Not only will this yield an authentic and effective public witness to an increasingly skeptical culture, but it will also bolster and strengthen the sort of liberalism and pluralism necessary for the continued success of the American political experiment.

---

50. Voting for a third or minor party is certainly an option for Christians dissatisfied with either major party candidate in a given election. But given our electoral and representative system, which provides single-member districts whose members are elected in a "first past the post" system, the emergence of a third party to challenge the hegemony of our two major parties is simply not feasible. Christians can vote for third parties, but we shouldn't expect them to challenge the status quo. See chapter 7 for more on this increasingly popular question.

51. Authorship of the song is unclear, though it is sometimes attributed to Albert Brumley, who also wrote the southern gospel hit "I'll Fly Away," made popular in the 2000 film *O Brother, Where Are Thou?*

5

Liberalism, Pluralism, and Christian Politics

"When you wed liberal democracy to intact families, strong civic engagement, and virtues of self-discipline and self-restraint, you can unleash prosperity and innovation unlike anything the world has seen before."[1]

I was at a faculty retreat along with a few dozen political scientists, economists, and historians from Christian colleges and universities when I had the idea for this book. During an afternoon session, I found myself weighing how Christians should think about our cultural and political engagement in a divided, polarized age. Inspired by disagreement with one of the retreat's speakers, I remember writing down a term on a piece of paper: *uneasy citizenship.*

That speaker was Patrick Deneen, a political scientist at Notre Dame and author of *Why Liberalism Failed.*[2] Deneen wrote that liberalism's focus on individual rights has paradoxically created an environment wholly unwelcoming and inhospitable to liberalism writ large—it has, he believes, become a victim of its own success. As a result, he argued America (and the West in general) has moved into a postliberal era, where culture, politics, and the state is no longer particularly friendly to the ideas of classical liberalism, such as free speech and protections for property. The solution, to

---

1. French, *Divided We Fall*, 182.
2. Deneen, *Why Liberalism Failed*.

Deneen and other post-liberals, is to seek a new governing framework for our political and social systems.

Rod Dreher, author of *The Benedict Option* and *Live Not By Lies*, is similarly pessimistic about the future of liberalism—again, not the ideology generally tied to the Democratic Party, but the framework for government and politics emphasizing individual liberty and limited government. "The unhappy truth," he wrote in a column for *The American Conservative*, "is that liberalism as we Americans have known it is probably dead."[3] Dreher was writing from Hungary, where he had come to admire its authoritarian president, Viktor Orban. Orban is no friend of liberalism, using his time as president to redraw electoral districts favorable to his party, reshape the country's courts in his image, and crack down on what he sees as unfair media coverage, among other things. In this same column, Dreher wrote,

> Our future is almost certainly going to be left-illiberal or right-illiberal. It's not the future I would prefer, but we are not being given a choice here. While the Establishment right, or what's left of it, pens its sixty-sixth pointless column denouncing Trumpism while back-door surrendering to soft totalitarianism, and while the MAGA hotheads dissipate their anger in futile performative gestures, the right-of-center thought leaders who want to figure out how to resist effectively will be coming to Budapest to observe, to talk, and to learn.

Dreher later argued that the state bears the responsibility for confronting "woke" ideologies and behaviors:

> Which is the only power capable of standing up to Woke Capitalists, as well as these illiberal leftists in academia, media, sports, cultural institutions, and other places? The state. That's it. This is disorienting to Anglo-American conservatives, who are accustomed to seeing the state as the enemy, and institutions of civil society, especially business, as friends of freedom. It's no longer true, and people on the Right who want to fight soft totalitarianism had better start to understand this.

A few months after Dreher's essay, the National Conservatism Conference—NatCon—held its annual meeting in Orlando, Florida. Speakers included Deneen and Dreher, plus elected officials like Ted Cruz, Josh Hawley, Marco Rubio, and J. D. Vance. The message of the meeting was clear: conservatism must aggressively fight back against an increasingly

---

3. Dreher, "Tucker To Hungary, Nixon To China."

hostile progressive agenda or inevitably be steamrolled by it. David Brooks observed and summarized the meeting in an essay for *The Atlantic*, titled "The Terrifying Future of the American Right."[4] He suggested that the future of American conservatism, as observed at one NatCon, should alarm conservatives who value limited government and individual liberties:

> This is national conservatism pursued to its logical conclusion: using state power to break up and humble the big corporations and to push back against coastal cultural values. The culture war merges with the economic-class war—and a new right emerges in which an intellectual cadre, the national conservatives, rallies the proletarian masses against the cultural/corporate elites. All your grandparents' political categories get scrambled along the way.

Not all conservatives, however, were alarmed by Brooks's account. Josh Hammer, a vocal supporter of the national conservatism movement, remarked that Brooks's description simply made the idea of this movement more appealing. "Sign me up!" Hammer concluded.[5]

For defenders of liberalism (including many conservatives), the notion that the state should be in the business of reining in certain viewpoints ought to be deeply troubling. After all, a government with the power to control and restrict your opponents' freedoms also has the power to control *your* freedoms. This is not to say that recent criticisms of liberalism are without foundation. Consider this from Jeff Bilbro:

> When the public sphere provided just one rather weak form of communal identity among many others—family, place, ethnic group, religious tradition—then its dynamics were muted. But as other forms of belonging and membership have eroded, the particular forms of community on offer through the public square become increasingly important and formative in people's lives.[6]

When major institutions fail, others inevitably emerge to fill the void. And in the United States, where a once rich tradition of civil religion and booming social capital has given way to the expressive individualism of identity politics and the demands of an unfettered and cold free market, the consequences are clear. Bilbro continues:

---

4. Brooks, "Terrifying Future of the American Right."
5. Hammer, "I Think @nytdavidbrooks Intended This to Be a Hit Piece."
6. Bilbro, *Reading the Times*, 126.

> When we belong less profoundly to our families, our places, and our religious traditions, we're more susceptible to being caught up in the secular, metaphorical, market-driven communities of the public sphere. Yet such forms of belonging are inadequate substitutes for thick, sustaining communities; they are better described as swarms of atomized individuals.[7]

While this conversation may seem academic, its consequences are real. A decline of social capital has led to an increasingly individualized society, where we are less and less dependent on our neighbors and institutions. Loneliness is on the rise, as is institutional skepticism and distrust. More and more, we have fewer and fewer things to bind us together.

All this has led to dissatisfaction with the framework underlying our social and political arrangements. This framework is *liberalism*, a philosophy of politics emphasizing individual rights and liberties, consent of the governed, the rule of law, and more. With its seeds in the writings of seventeenth-century political philosopher John Locke, liberalism has been the dominant sociopolitical framework in Western nations for centuries. Its influence on the values of the American Revolution and the Constitution is indelible. But for Patrick Deneen, liberalism's successes are leading to its downfall:

> A political philosophy that was launched to foster greater equity, defend a pluralist tapestry of different cultures and beliefs, protect human dignity, and, of course, expand liberty, in practice generates titanic inequality, enforces uniformity and homogeneity, fosters material and spiritual degradation, and undermines freedom. . . . To call for the cures of liberalism's ills by applying more liberal measures is tantamount to throwing gas on a raging fire. It will only deepen our political, social, economic, and moral crisis.[8]

Paradoxically, the challenges wrought by liberalism are only possible under liberalism. Its strengths have exposed its weaknesses. And for many, the solution to these challenges requires rethinking our liberal framework altogether.

Still, despite legitimate and serious concerns emanating from our liberal order for politics and culture, liberalism remains the best framework for ordering and structuring complex, pluralist, and free societies. Critics contend that liberalism inevitably leads to a people less prone to flourish,

---

7. Bilbro, *Reading the Times*, 127.
8. Deneen, *Why Liberalism Failed*, 4.

but people can only authentically flourish with the restraints on government and support for individual freedoms inherent to liberalism. Moreover, Christians should take steps to reinforce and strengthen liberal institutions and values, not only to respect our neighbors as made in the image of God, but also for self-preservation as we become more of a cultural minority in the years and decades ahead.

To draw on Winston Churchill, in this chapter I will argue that for Americans and for Christians, liberalism is the worst governing framework there is except for all the others. Christians concerned with the future of political engagement would be wise to support the American liberal tradition as an essential component of our uneasy citizenship.

DRAG QUEEN STORY HOUR, *BOSTOCK*, AND THE CASE AGAINST LIBERALISM

No story in recent years better highlights liberalism's alleged weaknesses than certain people reading books to children at public libraries. I am speaking, of course, of Drag Queen Story Hour (DQSH). First organized in San Francisco in 2015, DQSH has expanded to a loose network of non-profits around the country focused on the nexus of children's literacy and LGBTQ pride. Specifically, DQSH organizers say they are providing alternative children's programming to most public libraries' largely "heteronormative" events.[9] The goal for DQSH, they say, is not indoctrination, but an inclusive and welcoming space, including for families out of the cultural mainstream.

Not surprisingly, DQSH has drawn its share of attention, with supporters and opponents holding strong views about its role in American society. Those in favor of DQSH cite values of inclusion and kindness toward those different from the status quo, as well as new strategies for promoting literacy in children. In addition to these supporters, there are those who oppose DQSH on a moral basis but nevertheless support it for legal reasons, citing its protection under the First Amendment. David French, the lawyer and columnist, once described DQSH as "one of the blessings of liberty."[10] And while libertarian scholar Steven Greenhut called DQSH "bizarre," he believed that conservatives seeking to bar such events from

9. Kuga, "Some Libraries Are Facing Backlash Against LGBT Programs."

10. Wallace-Wells, "David French, Sohrab Ahmari, and the Battle for the Future of Conservatism."

public spaces were unwisely seeking to strengthen government to penalize unpopular views.[11]

Other opponents are less generous than French and Greenhut. They see DQSH as the latest instance of cultural backsliding into public immorality, with an emboldened and increasingly aggressive left explicitly targeting children with corrupt behaviors. Columnist Sohrab Ahmari is a leading voice of this perspective. "This is demonic," Ahmari said of DQSH in 2019.[12] Such events are not, he argues, among the blessings of liberty described by French, but rather lamentable yet predictable outcomes of a social framework—liberalism—emphasizing individual liberty above all else. Critically, Ahmari concludes:

> Conservative Christians can't afford these luxuries. Progressives understand that culture war means discrediting their opponents and weakening or destroying their institutions. Conservatives should approach the culture war with a similar realism. Civility and decency are secondary values. They regulate compliance with an established order and orthodoxy. We should seek to use these values to enforce our order and our orthodoxy, not pretend that they could ever be neutral. To recognize that enmity is real is its own kind of moral duty.[13]

For Ahmari, the solution for those concerned about DQSH is not simply to ignore them or attempt to persuade others to ignore them. Instead, it is to use the power of the state to enforce order and orthodoxy.

DQSH is certainly limited in scope, but for those skeptical of the current direction of liberalism in American society, it is a perfect example of this decline. It is, however, far from the only example. Consider also the US Supreme Court's 2020 decision in *Bostock v. Clayton County*.[14] In a 6–3 ruling authored by conservative Neil Gorsuch, the court held that the Civil Rights Act's prohibition on sex discrimination in employment also applies to sexual orientation and gender identity. As a result of this decision, sexual orientation and gender identity are protected classes on the same level as race, religion, and more, at least under federal law. In the same way that a supervisor cannot fire someone for being Black, he now cannot fire someone for being gay.

11. Greenhut, "Drag-Queen Debate Spotlights Creepy Trend on Right."
12. Goldberg, "Leave Drag Queen Story Hour Alone!"
13. Ahmari, "Against David French-Ism."
14. *Bostock v. Clayton County*, 590 U.S. 644.

Liberalism, Pluralism, and Christian Politics

The response to *Bostock* was deafening. Some praised the decision as a major development for strengthening and expanding LGBTQ rights.[15] Others—mainly conservatives—lamented the decision as creating unnecessary challenges for religious freedom and conscience rights.[16] For other conservative critics, though, *Bostock* was a reason to advance a new method of legal interpretation altogether, one that would lead to favorable legal outcomes for those critical of the classical liberal order.

This method is known as common good originalism (CGO). Originalism—with its emphasis on the meaning of constitutional and statutory language at the time the language was adopted—has been the preferred method of legal interpretation among conservatives for the past several decades, including all of the current conservative Supreme Court justices. CGO, on the other hand, would balance the meaning of the text with the principles of the American founding. The result, according to leading advocate Josh Hammer, would mean using the levers of government to advance the common good—defined by Hammer as not simply traditional ideas of marriage, sex, and gender but also more stringent immigration policies and content-based restrictions on speech.[17] While couched in general terms, in practice CGO would yield outcomes aligned with a very specific (and partisan) vision of public policy.

CGO did not emerge because of *Bostock*; indeed, debates over CGO and related theories of legal reasoning had been swirling for months, if not years, before Gorsuch's 2020 opinion. But just as DQSH has proved to be an attractive target for those critical of the excesses of liberalism, *Bostock* was the spark that launched the CGO project to new heights. If an originalist like Neil Gorsuch, the thinking went, could author a decision so anathema to conservative values as *Bostock*, then another direction is needed. And that direction, it became clear, should be less focused on means and more focused on ends.

DQSH and *Bostock* are just two recent examples of the growing case against liberalism. As Deneen wrote in *Why Liberalism Failed*, liberalism's success has proved to be its undoing. As more and more people become dissatisfied with our cultural trajectory, louder and louder voices are arguing not to persuade or redirect, but rather tear down and rebuild altogether. They say liberalism no longer works for the American people, including

---

15. Stern, "Neil Gorsuch Just Handed Down a Historic Victory for LGBTQ Rights."
16. Walker, "Bostock Is as Bad as You Think."
17. Hammer, "Common Good Originalism."

many Christians. It is time, they claim, for something else. In an essay following his book, Deneen wrote, "To those on the right and the left alike who insist that we need more freedom to cure the mischiefs of freedom, we should resoundingly respond: We won't be fooled again."[18]

One of these voices seeking a new framework is Rod Dreher. Over the years, Dreher has evolved from someone skeptical of the future of liberalism[19] to increasingly convinced that American society is heading inexorably toward a system of "soft totalitarianism."[20] Under this system, political institutions may be *technically* free and open, but conservatives and Christians will face oppression via cultural and corporate institutions. The solution must be for Christians to embrace a different framework that utilizes state power to stem the tide of incoming cultural persecution. As I wrote earlier in this chapter, Dreher's model for such engagement comes from Hungary: "With our own conservative establishment either neutered or sidelined by pointless lib-owning enthusiasms, thinkers of the American Right who actually care about saving our civilization ought to be coming to Hungary . . . and to make common cause with these people."[21]

True, Hungary's Viktor Orban has led the charge for legislation aimed at shoring up conservative values, including safeguarding traditional conceptions of sexuality and gender and passing nationalist policies concerning immigration. But the way he has done this is through chipping away at Hungary's liberal democratic institutions, using overwhelming control of the legislature to redraw legislative districts favorable to his party, rewarding allies with prominent positions in the public and private sectors, and even establishing new levels of courts favorable to his positions.[22] There are still free elections in Hungary, but it is increasingly difficult for dissenters to win. Political scientists call this "democratic backsliding" and "competitive authoritarianism." For Dreher, though, the crucial ends of "saving our civilization" more than justify Orban's illiberal means.

All this cuts to the heart of what critics believe is wrong with liberalism today. Liberalism may establish a framework where personal and economic freedom can thrive, but this does not always lead to human flourishing at an individual or collective level. People can choose for themselves under a

18. Deneen, "Good That Is Common."
19. Dreher, *Benedict Option*.
20. Dreher, *Live Not by Lies*.
21. Dreher, "Tucker To Hungary, Nixon To China."
22. Marantz, "Does Hungary Offer a Glimpse of Our Authoritarian Future?"

liberal order, but sometimes they make disordered and harmful choices. Free markets may lead to economic efficiency, but they can also hollow out communities. Importantly, liberalism's connection to religion and shared morality has been severed in favor of expressive individualism. And without shared principles, liberalism is destined to drift into moral relativism.

Far from being a force for good and human flourishing, critics see liberalism as empowering humanity's worst impulses. These critics see no point in preserving a collapsing social framework simply to maintain the status quo. The next step is to move away from the classical liberal tradition toward a framework better equipped to promote and sustain the common good. Furthermore, Christians should be among those ushering in a new and better environment, precisely because of the flourishing that comes with the gospel message. Our political engagement, critics say, should not be in the service of empty humanism but rather to promote a vision of the good life anchored in the truth of Christianity.[23]

THE CASE FOR LIBERALISM

More measured than Ahmari's and Deneen's postliberal caucus and Dreher's desire for illiberal conservatism, scholar Nathaniel Blake suggests a revision to liberalism that prioritizes the community over the individual. For Blake, the sacred cows of the liberal tradition—individual liberty and market economics—are not ends in themselves but rather a means to individual and collective flourishing. "Human flourishing and fulfillment require community, not atomistic individualism," Blake writes. "Free commerce . . . is an instrumental, rather than an intrinsic good."[24] Instead of calling for liberalism to be replaced by some fashionable and seemingly attractive alternative, Blake instead calls for it to be renewed and bolstered, much like a home in a state of disrepair can be renovated rather than demolished.

I am not naïve to the problems with or challenges of liberalism in our contemporary context. But, like Blake, I am increasingly convinced that the way forward is not a wholesale abandonment of the classical liberal tradition, but rather a shoring up and strengthening of liberalism as it exists

---

23. This could go as far as empowering the state to promote and enforce Christian principles through a form of "theocratic Caesarism." See, for example, Wolfe, *Case for Christian Nationalism*.

24. Blake, "For Americans To Have Freedom, They Must Revive The Common Good."

today. Not only does liberalism provide the best bulwark for Christians in a post-Christian society, but, as John Inazu writes, these frameworks are necessary for living together across deep differences.[25] Liberalism is not without its weaknesses, as its critics have made convincingly clear. But these weaknesses are not enough for Americans—and Christians—to abandon it altogether. Instead, we should seek to improve it as the best framework for human flourishing in a fallen world.

David French has emerged as one of the most ardent and persuasive defenders of liberalism. In a 2019 debate with Sohrab Ahmari about the future of liberalism, French stated that while procedural liberalism—wherein our political systems enforce fair rules that treat people equally—may sometimes yield outcomes we disagree with, it nevertheless "keeps everyone at the table" in a diverse and contested society. Under this system, persuasion, not coercion, matters most.[26] Ahmari's complaints about liberalism, French argued, largely stem from dissatisfaction with outcomes, not processes. The solution must not be to abandon the liberal project altogether but to make better arguments about human flourishing and the common good under this framework.

More important for us is French's *Christian* defense of the liberal tradition. In an essay motivated by increasing opposition to liberalism on the American left and right, French cited two values inherent to American liberalism Christians should be defending.[27] First is the "God-given dignity of man" established in the Declaration of Independence and the Constitution. He wrote:

> The liberties recognized in these key documents are worthy not because we are good—or because we always exercise them in virtuous ways—but because we are *valuable*. And so the rights to speak, to exercise your faith, to be free from cruel and unusual punishments, to be liberated from arbitrary exercises of state power, and to enjoy equal protection under the law all proclaim a secular version of a divine truth—each person is of incalculable worth.

In the earliest pages of the Bible, God declares that humans are made in his image. These foundational American principles declare this truth in practical, tangible ways, embodying timeless natural rights in ways previously unseen in the history of governing institutions. And while French is

---

25. Inazu, *Confident Pluralism.*
26. Leeman, "Conservatives Clash on the Goal of Government."
27. French, "Christian Defense of American Classical Liberalism."

quick to concede that these values are not always realized in practice—he has highlighted historical abuses toward racial minorities[28] and recent injustices toward conservative Christians[29] as examples—these errors do not demand a wholesale rejection of the liberal project.

Second, the Declaration and Constitution "recognize and seek to mitigate the inherent sinfulness of man." French continued, "American history combined with American ideals demonstrates that limiting governmental authority is vital to respecting human dignity, in large part because there is no class of person who can be entirely trusted to rule." As a political scientist, I wholeheartedly concur. Whenever I teach my American Government and Politics class, I emphasize that checks and balances and the separation of powers inherent to our constitutional structure make little sense absent the understanding that human beings are fallen people. Those skeptical of liberalism on the left and the right have a loftier vision of governance than liberals do, aiming to establish a system whereby government is empowered to a far greater degree. With our understanding of humanity's sinful nature, Christians should know better than to entertain these utopian visions.

Beyond an appeal to America's founding principles, Christians ought to support liberalism as a means of encouraging pluralism. I define pluralism as a framework of politics and culture marked by competing (and even contradictory) conceptions of the good life.[30] Pluralism means that government and culture ought to respect and embolden different ideas to thrive and compete with one another. Writing in *Federalist 10,* James Madison argued for pluralism as a primary solution to factional conflict in the developing United States.[31] Madison wrote that by encouraging the spread of factions and different perspectives, it becomes less likely for one group to consistently dominate others in a competitive democratic system. As Christians, we can remain confident in the truth of our beliefs while giving space for other points of view to exist.

While acknowledging the practical importance of pluralism as a governing framework, Michael Wear argues for pluralism from an explicitly Christian perspective. He believes that pluralism is not just about passive tolerance or a hands-off libertarianism toward our neighbors. Instead, pluralism means acknowledging that our neighbors with whom we disagree

---

28. French, "American Racism."
29. French, "Punitive Intolerance Is No Way to Preserve Pluralism."
30. Bennett, "In Pluralism's Defense."
31. Madison, "Federalist 10."

are made in God's image and should thus be afforded the same rights we seek for ourselves. "In a healthy pluralistic society," he once wrote, "we will resist the urge to control and coerce using whatever power is at our disposal," continuing that those committed to pluralism must be "prepared to sacrifice maximal advantage for the good of the whole, even those we do not understand."[32] Pluralism may be messy and inefficient compared to alternatives, but this does not negate its importance for diverse and complex societies.

Though the Supreme Court's *Bostock* decision drew its share of critics, others saw the ruling as a positive step toward practical pluralism. Mark Rienzi, president of the Becket Fund for Religious Liberty, is one of these voices. Though no fan of the decision itself, Rienzi ultimately recognized *Bostock*, as written, makes ample room for differing perspectives. "The heavy focus on religious liberty in a case that did not present the question," Rienzi wrote, "strongly suggests that the six-justice *Bostock* majority understands that the Constitution and federal law provide strong protections for the rights of religious entities to act in accordance with their beliefs."[33] Rienzi went on to argue that other recent decisions show the court "systematically building precedent on the foundational idea that religious freedom can help people in a diverse, pluralistic society live together in peace—even amid deep disagreements over fundamental issues."

I couldn't agree more. In an essay for *Christianity Today* following the *Bostock* opinion, I wrote that the court could use this decision (and others that have followed) to identify compromises between religious liberty and LGBTQ rights other branches of government have been unable to do. Referencing stalled legislative compromises, I wrote, "It is not difficult to see how the basic ideas of the proposal could be enacted via a series of judicial rulings, especially under the current composition of the court."[34] And while the 2022 Respect for Marriage Act included a healthy dose of protections for religious institutions opposed to same-sex marriage,[35] the courts remain a likely source of protections for pluralism in the years to come.

In addition to fostering pluralism, our liberal order also ensures robust protections for religious freedom. At first glance, it might seem counterintuitive for Christians to support religious freedom, given our belief

32. Wear, "Power and Sacrifice."
33. Rienzi, "Symposium."
34. Bennett, "LGBT Rights Ruling Isn't the Beginning of the End for Religious Liberty."
35. Esbeck, "Everything You Need to Know About the Respect for Marriage Act."

that Jesus is the way, the truth, and the life. Why, some might ask, should we support people making wrong choices, especially wrong choices with eternal consequences? Simply, Christians can be confident in the truth of Jesus and the hope we have in him without needing to coerce our neighbors to the good news of the gospel. This is not a new doctrine; none other than church father Tertullian expressed this belief in the third century.[36] Joshua Wester puts it well: "Religious freedom is a critical and thoroughly Christian doctrine. It is sacred and must always be protected."[37]

As Christianity's influence in the public square continues to decline opposite increasing secularism, Andrew Walker notes the importance of religious freedom moving forward. "Contestability," he writes, "should be one of Christianity's most cherished principles as its influence wanes, as it allows for continued dialogue and Christian public witness."[38] Yes, Christians should support religious freedom for theological reasons, as Walker argues in his book *Liberty for All*. But we should also support religious freedom to ensure Christianity can continue to thrive in a post-Christian society. Opposing rights for religious minorities today—such as a Muslim group seeking to build a mosque[39] or a Native American group seeking to protect its land[40]—will only hinder the spread of Christianity in the long term.

Among Christians, supporting religious freedom should not be a political or partisan wedge issue. Tony Perkins, president of the conservative Family Research Council and chair of the US Commission on International Religious Freedom, has extolled the virtues of robust religious freedom not just for Christians, but for religions around the world. He recounted abuses toward religious minorities in China, Iran, and Russia—none of them Christians—and argued his Christian beliefs command him to pray for their freedom to believe and practice their traditions and faiths. "Religious freedom is not merely an American right," Perkins wrote for Religion News Service. "It is a human right that we are compelled to protect and promote for all people of all faiths everywhere."[41]

---

36. Wilken, *Liberty in the Things of God*.
37. Wester, "Why Would Christians Support Religious Freedom?"
38. Walker, *Liberty for All*, 183.
39. Strode, "ERLC's Moore Defends Religious Freedom for Muslims."
40. Moore and Goodrich, "How Eagle Feathers and Copper Mines Might Alter Your Religious Liberty."
41. Perkins, "Why Christians Must Support Religious Freedom for Everyone."

Similarly, despite what evangelical theologian Matthew Kaemingk calls the "scandalous particularities" of the Christian faith—in which there is no equating false traditions with the truth of the gospel—he reads Scripture as requiring a commitment to religious freedom and pluralism. Why? Because Jesus opened the door for us when we were in opposition to God in our sin. "I'm going to make public space for my Muslim neighbor because the cross of the Galilean made space for me," Kaemingk writes. "I can't enter public life any other way."[42] Likewise, attorney Luke Goodrich has a simple explanation for why Christians ought to defend religious freedom: "We were created in the image of God for relationship with Him, but we can't have an authentic relationship with Him unless we also have the freedom to embrace or reject Him."[43]

I serve on the board of directors of Neighborly Faith (NF), an educational ministry aimed at improving dialogue between evangelical Christians and their Muslim and other non-Christian neighbors. NF hosts conferences on college campuses and organizes events with speakers of different faiths to show that people can disagree on issues as important as religion yet cultivate meaningful relationships in our communities. As a college professor, I can attest to the value of these interactions, especially in terms of preparing our graduates to move into an increasingly diverse world. On a simpler note, NF co-founder Kevin Singer hopes for a world where more American evangelicals have Muslim friends. "That would be amazing," he told Religion News Service.[44]

Singer's vision is not naivete or moral relativism; it is the gospel in action. Moreover, it is the essence of pluralism made feasible by liberalism. Far from perfect, liberalism affords opportunities for cross-cultural dialogue and friendships essential for learning, outreach, and, yes, evangelism. Under liberalism, minority views are not cowed into silence; they are allowed to develop in a marketplace of diversity and interact with competing and contradictory views. Just as Elijah proclaimed the truth of God on Mount Carmel,[45] so too can Christians today interact with a skeptical world fully confident in the truth of the gospel. Liberalism is not an impediment to our faith; it is a framework that allows our faith to thrive.

---

42. Kaemingk, "Making America Hospitable for Religious Outsiders."
43. Goodrich, *Free to Believe*, 23.
44. Miller, "Neighborly Faith Urges Evangelicals to Find a 'third Way.'"
45. 1 Kings 18:20–40.

AN ASIDE ON CHRISTIAN NATIONALISM AND NATIONAL CONSERVATIVISM

In 2018 two sociologists and a psychologist published an article in the academic journal *Sociology of Religion*. The paper, titled "Make America Christian Again: Christian Nationalism and Voting for Donald Trump in the 2016 Presidential Election," was not the first academic study of Christian nationalism (CN) in the United States, but given its conclusions about the role CN played in the election of Donald Trump, it attracted a great deal of attention beyond the journal's traditionally narrow academic audience.[46]

The article examined questions from the 2017 Baylor Religion Survey alluding to CN, including those measuring agreement with the following statements: "The federal government should declare the United States a Christian nation," "The federal government should advocate Christian values," "The federal government should allow the display of religious symbols in public spaces," and "The success of the United States is part of God's plan." In analyzing this data they made what became an important—and hotly contested—conclusion: "We find strong evidence that Christian nationalism played an important role in predicting which Americans voted for Donald Trump."[47]

These scholars would publish other articles and books about CN and its influence on Americans' political attitudes.[48] And while these studies offered plenty for other scholars to criticize,[49] the debate over CN eventually outgrew its academic environment and spawned a larger cultural conversation. Christians wrote books on CN, both criticizing[50] and defending[51] its place in American society. National media, from *Meet the Press*[52] to NPR[53] to

---

46. Whitehead, Perry, and Baker, "Make America Christian Again."

47. Whitehead, Perry, and Baker, "Make America Christian Again," 164.

48. See, for example, Whitehead and Perry, "A More Perfect Union?"; Perry and Whitehead, "Christian Nationalism and White Racial Boundaries"; Whitehead, Schnabel, and Perry, "Gun Control in the Crosshairs"; Perry, Whitehead, and Grubbs, "Culture Wars and COVID-19 Conduct"; Whitehead and Perry, *Taking America Back for God*; Gorski and Perry, *Flag and the Cross*.

49. Hall, "Tilting at Windmills."

50. See, for example, Miller, *Religion of American Greatness*.

51. Wolfe, *Case for Christian Nationalism*.

52. Marquez, "Rise of Theocracy among Conservatives."

53. Burnett, "Christian Nationalism Is Still Thriving."

Fox News,[54] covered CN and its role in American culture. CN even found its way to the halls of American government: The Congressional Freethought Congress—comprised primarily by Democrats—held a briefing on the dangers CN poses to American democracy,[55] while some Republicans in the House of Representatives and beyond defended CN's role in American public life.[56] Meanwhile, scholar Mark David Hall is skeptical of the attention CN has received. "Christian nationalism," he wrote, "is an amorphous concept that is primarily used to tar Christians who are motivated by their faith to advocate for policies that critics don't like."[57]

CN is difficult to define because opponents and proponents disagree about what exactly it is. That said, I prefer Paul Miller's definition: "The unique feature of Christian nationalism is that it defines America as a Christian nation and it wants the government to promote a specific Anglo-Protestant cultural template as the official culture of the country."[58] Considering this narrow yet inclusive definition, those equating any faith-based political action—particularly from conservative Christians—with CN misunderstand the relationship between faith and politics and minimize the danger of actual CN to liberalism, pluralism, and religious freedom.

Of course, some do not see any danger at all. Stephen Wolfe, who holds a PhD in political theory from Louisiana State University, is the author of *The Case for Christian Nationalism*. Wolfe combines political philosophy, theology, and cultural analysis to argue that CN is not only an acceptable framework for civic life but preferable to alternatives like liberalism and pluralism. Yet not all conservatives find Wolfe's arguments compelling. Pastor and author Kevin DeYoung—who, like Wolfe, is a Presbyterian and Reformed in his theology—wrote a critical review of Wolfe's project, labeling it "right-wing wokeism" and "not a nationalism that honors and represents the name of Christ."[59] Toward the end of his lengthy review, DeYoung wrote,

> Biblical instincts are better than nationalist ones, and the ethos of the Christian Nationalism project fails the biblical smell test. Will the person who goes all in on this book . . . be apt to grow in faith,

54. Parks, "Media Meltdown over Supreme Court Ruling.'"
55. Jenkins, "Scholars, Activists Brief Lawmakers on Role of Christian Nationalism."
56. Jenkins, "Republicans Mostly Mum."
57. Hall, "Tilting at Windmills."
58. Kristian, "Is There an Alternative to Christian Nationalism?"
59. DeYoung, "Rise of Right-Wing Wokeism."

hope, and love? Will he be led to rejoice insofar as he shares in Christ's sufferings? And if the end of things is at hand, will he be self-controlled and sober-minded for the sake of his prayers? Or will this book help us return reviling for reviling?

For DeYoung, the answer is clear: CN is not the answer for Christians disappointed with the direction of American politics and culture.

What are Christians to do with this debate? Andrew Walker has encouraged Christians to be precise in their motives and arguments when discussing CN.[60] Speaking to those supportive of CN, Walker writes, "Convince me this isn't just a theology used to sacralize the culture or impose exclusionary political power." And writing to those wary of CN, Walker asks, "Convince me you have a political theology that isn't . . . high on pietism but averse to wielding political power for the common good." It is possible for Christians to want to influence public policy in accordance with our faith without wanting to institutionalize our faith via government power. Christians can act faithfully within our society's liberal framework while remaining committed to our convictions.

Similar to CN, the rise of national conservatism (NatCon) is another recent challenge to liberalism. Growing in popularity following Donald Trump's successful run for president in 2016, NatCon argues for a more aggressive conservatism to counter what its sympathizers see as an emboldened and increasingly hostile progressivism. While traditional conservatism is generally wary of government power, NatCon assumes that government can be an effective ally and weapon against one's ideological opponents.[61] Writing about NatCon's support for Hungary's Viktor Orban, the *New York Times*'s Elisabeth Zerofsky explains that Orban is seen as supporting true freedom, one where "no online vigilante mob is waiting to deprive people of their livelihood for uttering a wrong word."[62]

Not surprisingly, those on the left dismiss NatCon as a dangerous ideology threatening the fabric of the American political system. But NatCon

---

60. Walker, "What Does 'Christian Nationalism' Even Mean?"

61. In NatCon's official statement of principles the movement argues that "in those states or subdivisions in which law and justice have been manifestly corrupted, or in which lawlessness, immorality, and dissolution reign, national government must intervene energetically to restore order." Of course, "lawlessness" and "immorality" are not objective terms, raising the question of who determines to use the national government as a cudgel. For NatCon, the answer is obvious. See The American Conservative, "National Conservatism."

62. Zerofsky, "How the American Right Fell in Love With Hungary."

also has critics on the right, seeing its desires to wield government power and interfere in the free market as deeply flawed and dangerous. Yes, the online mob is real, but the solution is not to empower the government to stomp it out. Though perhaps appealing in the moment, the long-term implications of such empowerment pose real concerns for civil liberties like speech and association. Conservatives are also wary of the government having such influence in regulating culture. "I don't want bureaucrats in Washington, DC, to develop a blueprint of the correct form of national culture we're supposed to identify with," wrote Paul Miller. "Any effort to do so will inevitably, and justifiably, backfire."[63]

There is also a sound Christian argument against NatCon. In an essay for *First Things*, Peter Leithart criticized NatCon's emphasis on national values while minimizing Christian values. "It's difficult to shake the sense," Leithart said, "that National Conservatism instrumentalizes Scripture, appealing to it not as the word of the Creator God but as a wellspring of national values."[64] He continued, "The church, not the nation, is the telos of political life; without the universal truth to which the church bears witness and which she embodies, nations don't know what they're for." In *Reason*, Stephanie Slade cited Matthew 5 in writing, "There's nothing Christian about the idea that we should hope not to convert or persuade but to defeat and destroy our ideological opponents. To gain the whole world and lose your soul is no victory at all."[65]

NatCon, like CN, may be appealing in an increasingly contested culture, especially its promises to promote a vision of the common good to aid in our collective flourishing. It may also appeal to us due to its promise to make things easier for conservatives and Christians in our political and social engagement. This is not, however, what Christians were promised. In Mark 13, Jesus tells his disciples they would be hated because of him,[66] and in John 16 Jesus foretells tribulation for his people.[67] Thankfully, this is not the end of the story: we can take heart, for our savior has overcome the world. We need not put our trust in princes who cannot save.[68] Our confidence in a risen savior must be enough to sustain us during defeats

63. Miller, "Against 'Conservative Democracy.'"
64. Leithart, "Against National Conservatism."
65. Slade, "New Theocrats Are Neither Conservative Nor Christian."
66. Mark 13:13.
67. John 16:33.
68. Psalm 146:3.

and setbacks under our pluralist liberal framework. This is not defeatist; this is hope of the highest order.

THE ROAD AHEAD

A commitment to liberalism means accepting that we will all lose at some point. Following the 2020 presidential election, I wrote about the importance of losing well in American politics.[69] The legitimacy of elections is crucial to the legitimacy of the government, and by extension, our entire political system; if people are accustomed to rejecting electoral outcomes they don't like, then a collapse in our political system is not far behind. "Self-government depends," I wrote, "on citizens losing well with an eye toward the next election, not burning the system to the ground." Throwing out more than two centuries of practice following the disappointment of one election or defeat in one Supreme Court decision is not good practice. And for Christians, this not good orthopraxy.

Our confidence in Christ cannot be shaken through temporary setbacks in elections, policymaking, or judicial rulings. If this trust is inconsistent from election to election—if we begin to believe that only officials we support are ordained by God, while others deserve not only condemnation but full disobedience at every turn—then it is a weak and unstable trust. Deeply rooted hope in Jesus means trusting his provision in the worst of times. "If Christians should make peace with losing for the sake of our *humility*," I continued, "we should also do so to grow our *resilience*. Our response to defeat is a truer testament to our hope in Christ than our response to victory."

In a moving essay on the future of liberalism among Christians, author Jake Meador offered a stark reminder of the road ahead:

> We should be open to exile if the only other choice set before us is to betray the sober calling of Christian discipleship and the yoke of Christ put on us that calls us toward love of God and love of neighbor. If the cost of contending for our neighbors, all our neighbors, is exile then so be it. We might be pariahs for a season in the halls of American power, but given what those halls do and promote, is that such a loss? If a man gain the whole world and lose his own soul, what does it profit him? If the cost of fidelity to

---

69. Bennett, "We Need to Be Better Losers."

our Lord is exile, even martyrdom, then that is not a cost too high for the reward set before us.[70]

Christians should not actively seek exile, nor should we welcome political defeat. Faithful political engagement should be strategic and thoughtful, seeking to win for the betterment of our communities. But this engagement must not betray where our eternal citizenship lies. We ought not abandon a framework that honors the dignity of persons and places meaningful limits on our sinful natures just because it leads to occasionally unfavorable circumstances. Our political engagement must take a longer view.

I wrote in chapter 3 that the challenges facing Christians in the years ahead are real. And while the political engagement outlined in chapter 4 affords real opportunities to respond to these challenges, there are practical things we can do in the coming years to prepare—namely, to invest in meaningful and thick institutions and communities. With a better political engagement outlined and a defense of liberalism established, it is to these practical solutions we can now confidently turn.

---

70. Meador, "End of the Liberalism Debate."

6

Investing in Institutions

"The decisions we make today will be the determining factors for how we are in twenty-five years."[1]

"No, not *that* John Brown."

I have lost track of how many times I have said this, usually when meeting somebody for the first time and sharing where I work. *That* John Brown was the militant abolitionist, whose violent advocacy against slavery included leading elements of "Bloody Kansas"—including murdering pro-slavery settlers—and a raid on a federal armory in Virginia for the purpose of arming and inspiring a slave insurrection. Brown was ultimately caught, tried, convicted, and hanged.

Our John Brown—the namesake of John Brown University—was the evangelist who spread the gospel via a series of radio stations before, in 1919, founding a college on the Arkansas-Oklahoma border. Founded as a work college, where students would work jobs on campus in exchange for instruction, JBU eventually evolved into a liberal arts[2] university aimed at educating young men and women in a well-rounded and unapologetic Christian fashion. JBU's model of "Head, Heart, and Hand" speaks to the

---

1. Hoogstra, personal interview.

2. The liberal arts, as an intellectual tradition, formed the foundation of Western education for centuries, and included a broad study of the sciences (natural and social), arts, and humanities. A liberal arts education emphasizes intellectual curiosity and development more than the acquisition of specific skills—that is, prioritizing learning for the sake of learning as an essential component of a person's development.

mission of many distinctly Christian universities in today's environment, where students are not only given a college education but also spiritual development and opportunities for practical service.

I have been involved in Christian higher education for all but eight years since graduating high school. I have seen firsthand the benefits of Christian higher education in equipping students to be not just leaders in their communities and industries but also ambassadors for God's kingdom in a world increasingly skeptical of the good news of Jesus. Done well, Christian higher education does not just provide professional training and academic credentials; it helps students discover and cultivate their identity as Christians in a fallen world.

That said, Christian higher education is nearing a major crossroads. For most of our country's history Christianity was either embraced or at least tolerated; today the mood has begun to sour. As I described in chapter 3, our increasingly post-Christian society is starting to see the traditional Christian ethic and mission as anathema to prevailing cultural sensibilities. For Christian colleges and universities, this means facing criticism and even lawsuits[3] for maintaining hiring and student conduct standards rooted in a conservative understanding of gender and sexuality. Coupled with declining enrollments due to lower birthrates and other demographic challenges, Christian higher education is largely struggling even among its most financially secure institutions.[4]

When Rod Dreher wrote *The Benedict Option*[5] it was often interpreted as a call for Christians to withdraw from the public square and retreat into isolated communities, to separate from a declining culture increasingly hellbent on eradicating any semblance of conservative religious orthodoxy. I did not read *The Benedict Option* this way, nor did Dreher intend it as such. Instead, Dreher's argument stems from how American Christians have for generations been so focused on trying to transform the broader culture that we have neglected to maintain our own houses—namely, our churches and our distinctly Christian institutions, such as colleges and nonprofits.

Given the challenges outlined in this book, Christians should prioritize investing in our institutions as an essential element of our uneasy citizenship. I am not suggesting that we turn our attention solely inward, rejecting political and cultural engagement as ineffective or even worthless

---

3. Redden, "Religious Freedom vs. Freedom From Discrimination."
4. Cassetto, Worley, and Huiskes, "College to Reduce Faculty, Staff."
5. Dreher, *Benedict Option*.

compared to the work of strengthening our own communities. But a reorientation is definitely necessary, especially when our focus on national politics usually outweighs our attention to local concerns and when expressive individualism[6] and moralistic therapeutic deism[7] are increasingly alluring idols.

Simply put, Christians concerned with engaging politics and culture must first fortify our own spaces. This includes churches, especially at a moment when political, cultural, and geographic divisions are cleaving congregations and wreaking havoc on our Christian communities. This also includes Christian schools and colleges, not as required alternatives to public education but as institutions increasingly useful for discipleship and formation of young Christians. And it means committing to unity in the body of Christ—not downplaying or ignoring important points of disagreement among us as Christians, but approaching these debates with charity and grace. Embracing our uneasy citizenship is not just an individual endeavor; in this chapter, I show how we must do this collectively.

INVESTING IN CHURCHES

When people ask me about my testimony—how I came to know Jesus—I am reminded of my upbringing in the church. My testimony is not centered on a particular moment or series of events culminating with a bolt of realization of who Jesus is and how he died for me. Instead, I was raised in a supportive and vibrant church, and there isn't a time in my life I remember not knowing the good news of the gospel. I used to be embarrassed about my relatively tame testimony, at times even wondering whether my faith was legitimate absent a dramatic story to tell. But after someone once asked me what kind of testimony I would want my kids to have, my perspective changed. I am thankful to have had the Christian experience I did, rooted solidly in a local church and surrounded by a community of imperfect yet committed believers.

Christian churches are integral to the American story and experience. For centuries Americans have had the freedom to gather openly with other believers and worship, study, and commune with one another in the presence of the Holy Spirit. But as religiosity in the United States declines—in

---

6. Trueman, *Rise and Triumph of the Modern Self*.
7. Smith and Denton, *Soul Searching*.

terms of behavior, belief, and belonging[8]—churches are inevitably affected. Mainline Protestant traditions have seen drops in membership and attendance for decades, and there is evidence that this trend will soon extend to evangelical congregations. Ryan Burge, a leading scholar of religion, politics, and society in the United States, is pessimistic about the future of certain evangelical denominations, given the average age of their members. Nearly 70 percent of those in the Lutheran Church Missouri Synod are over 55, as are 57 percent of Southern Baptists.[9]

On a podcast with *The Gospel Coalition*'s Colin Hansen, Burge suggested many evangelical churches will soon be facing dire circumstances for other reasons:

> Listen, you see where the Mainline are right now? That's where you're going to be in ten or fifteen or twenty years. Here's the difference, though: a lot of Mainline traditions have no people but they have a ton of money. A lot of evangelical traditions are not as wealthy. . . . Episcopalians can live on life support for years, because they can keep the lights on. A lot of evangelical traditions, if they start dying off quickly, do not have that financial lifeline to keep them around for a long time.[10]

Despite consistent membership and attendance declines, most Mainline congregations have survived thanks to their denominations' historically deep pockets. Most evangelical traditions—especially nondenominational churches—simply do not have the financial legacy needed to keep them afloat amid rising secularization and declining church attendance, especially among younger Americans.

The decline of churches is not just a spiritual crisis. America's religious marketplace benefits not just religious Americans, but *everyone*. According to two Harvard researchers, religious communities provide myriad health and social benefits: "Something about the communal religious experience seems to matter. Something powerful takes place there, something that enhances health and well-being," they write. "The data are clear: Going to church remains central to true human flourishing."[11] And this is to say nothing of the resulting fall of social capital inevitably accompanying

---

8. Friesen and Wagner, "Beyond the 'Three Bs.'"
9. Burge, "I Don't Think People Fully Grasp."
10. Hansen and Burge, "Why Americans Quit Church."
11. VanderWeele and Case, "Empty Pews Are an American Public Health Crisis."

religious decline. Despite their imperfections and flaws, churches and religious communities provide a great benefit to American society.

Declining religious attendance is not the only challenge facing churches as we move further into the twenty-first century. In chapter 3, I referenced Carl Trueman's discussion of expressive individualism in the West and its increasing prevalence in our lives. As a reminder, expressive individualism means people emphasizing aspects of their identity—including gender and sexual orientation, race, and even religion—as essential to understanding who they are, even though these identities are becoming less and less rooted in anything substantively lasting and meaningful. And while churches may be tempted by the idol of expressive individualism in an attempt to maintain relevance in the years ahead, arguably more threatening is the allure of *moralistic therapeutic deism*.

Coined by sociologists Christian Smith and Melinda Lundquist Denton in a 2005 book, moralistic therapeutic deism (MTD) is a belief system emphasizing the importance of leading a good and moral life, providing positive and therapeutic benefits to adherents, and describing God as not particularly involved in one's daily life apart from blessing people who lead good and moral lives.[12] Despite MTD's incongruities with biblical Christianity, I'd wager you can find tenets of MTD proclaimed at any number of American churches on any given Sunday. Drawing people to the pews, the lie goes, is easier with more entertainment and uplifting sermons and less emphasis on the realities of sin and Jesus's call for sacrificial servanthood. MTD may "run counter to the gospel of Jesus Christ in every way,"[13] but fog machines, funny skits, and sermons that make us feel good about ourselves in the shallowest of ways often draw bigger crowds.

What are Christians to do in the face of such challenges to our churches? If my experience with Christian college students is any indication, we must commit to building up and investing in churches centered on a robust exegetical examination of God's word. Our cultural moment demands a richness in church teachings that rejects the temptation to scratch the "itching ears" of our self-centered attention spans.[14] Recent generations of Christians have grown up in churches focused on topical and thematic

12. Smith and Denton, *Soul Searching*.
13. Cosby, "Moralistic Therapeutic Deism."
14. 2 Timothy 4:3. In his March 19, 2023, sermon on this passage, Pastor Ted Wenger reminded the congregation of Redeemer Presbyterian Church in Siloam Springs, Arkansas of the wayward tendencies of our hearts and minds. "We are," he acknowledged, "vulnerable people."

sermons with an emphasis on entertainment, primarily (if subconsciously) as a way of drawing regular attenders. And though appealing at face value, the Christian students I encounter who take their faith seriously want something deeper, something authentic, something *more*. They can get their entertainment elsewhere; they make a commitment to attend church desiring to be fed.

This does not mean that all churches must follow the same model moving forward. Different communities will invariably have different needs. Geography, demographics, socioeconomics, and pastors' spiritual gifts all play a role in determining why churches have traditionally thrived. Moreover, it is true that Sunday worship resembling rock concerts and sermons emphasizing daily life over biblical exegesis may have been an effective ministry strategy in Aaron Renn's positive or neutral worlds. In earlier years, Christianity was the default moral compass for millions of people. Churches therefore may have felt the freedom to be creative in their structures and practices as a way to reach people familiar with the contours of Christianity, but not much else about the faith.

Our current moment, however, presents a new set of challenges for churches tasked with both reaching the lost and feeding the flock. Declining church attendance and membership, coupled with major cultural changes at best dismissive and at worst hostile to Christianity, means Christians should be shoring up churches dedicated to spiritual training and disciplines found exclusively in God's holy and inspired word. As our pool of churches shrinks, churches must be fully committed to biblical interpretation and exegesis as an antidote to a culture in greater and greater need of the good news of Jesus. This doesn't mean churches must be stuffy or stodgy to be faithful, rejecting anything contemporary in worship and aesthetics. But moving forward, our churches' priorities ought to be more carefully and rightly ordered, and we must support these priorities.

Christians can also commit to churches serving as essential bodies for discipleship in cultural and political matters. As people living in a community, everything we do—or don't do—has political implications. The same is true of churches and church leaders. Referencing a salient political issue from the pulpit is political, but so too is not speaking about it. And those in attendance are taking notice. For example, research from Neighborly Faith found that young evangelicals—including white evangelicals and people of color—routinely look to religious leaders for leadership on public issues and pay attention to these leaders' voices on political and cultural matters.[15] Churches and church leaders may shy away from addressing critical issues of the day for fear of creating division in the pews, but silence can have similarly divisive effects. "Maybe our political discipleship is malformed," writes Patrick Schreiner in *Political Gospel*, "because we don't think of our church as a *political* assembly."[16]

There are, of course, wrong ways to go about this. Sunday worship need not transform into political rallies or replace exegesis and hermeneutics with punditry. Writing for *The Gospel Coalition*, Matthew Hawkins encourages church leaders to make political discipleship a natural and regular element of the congregation's rhythm of life. "Regular practices," Hawkins writes, "help pastors avoid feeling like they have to shoehorn some special commentary into a Sunday morning service after an intense news cycle."[17] Sunday mornings can be the setting for this discipleship, yes, but so too can church-sponsored panel discussions and study groups, especially those that model charitable disagreements on salient and contentious issues.

What does it mean for Christians to invest in the kinds of churches best equipped to prepare us for embracing the tension inherent at the intersection of our faith and political engagement? It means committing to a congregation where the Bible is held in reverence, not simply as an instruction manual to prepare people for their upcoming week—or, worse yet, as a means to an end of confirming each of our political opinions. It means supporting pastors and other church leaders, especially during moments of heightened political tensions in our communities. It means holding our political opinions tight, but not tighter than the relationships we foster in diverse and imperfect congregations. Above all, it means committing to a church not that makes us most politically comfortable, but that helps us mature so we can flourish and better engage in an increasingly messy, pluralistic society.

"God didn't call us to live this life alone," my friend Dave Carroll writes. "No, He calls us to live it in community with one another, holding each other accountable, loving each other through our messiness."[18] As cultural Christianity in the United States continues its inexorable slide into irrelevance, our churches must be more intentional in political

---

15. Stackaruk and Singer, "Who Is Influencing Young Evangelicals on Politics?"
16. Schreiner, *Political Gospel*, 88.
17. Hawkins, "Why We Need the Church to Disciple Our Politics."
18. Carroll, "Church Is Messy."

discipleship, preparing Christians for a faithful and refreshing presence in an increasingly foreign culture. And for our part, Christians must encourage these churches in their difficult yet necessary work.

INVESTING IN CHRISTIAN EDUCATION

It might seem self-interested of me to dedicate a section of this chapter to the importance of investing in Christian education—particularly higher education. After all, I draw a (modest) paycheck from such a university and have spent more than half my life in higher education, as an undergraduate student, graduate student, lecturer, and professor. The truth is, after almost twenty years as a student and educator—half of that in deliberately Christian institutions—I am increasingly convinced of the necessary role Christian education plays in preparing young men and women of faith to encounter an increasingly secular world. As Christians adjust to occupying a smaller and likely less influential sphere of American culture, we must shore up and invest in the sorts of institutions that equip eager and hungry young minds to engage the world in faithful, effective ways.

For thirteen years, through elementary, middle, and high school, I was educated in public schools in Beaverton, Oregon. My teachers were generally caring, fair, and committed to their work. I was not indoctrinated or targeted for my Christian beliefs. I met people from different backgrounds and belief systems and learned how to live in and engage our country's pluralist culture. I played the trombone through middle and high school, played intramural basketball with friends, and worked behind the scenes for our high school's spring musicals. Mine was, by and large, a fine experience.

My first exposure to Christian education came as a freshman student at George Fox University. Nestled about halfway between Portland and the Oregon coast in the Willamette Valley's wine country, George Fox has its origins in the Quaker tradition. And while it still has affiliations with the Northwest Yearly Meeting of Friends, George Fox is best described as broadly evangelical, with faculty and students from myriad backgrounds of American evangelical Protestantism and Catholicism. It is big enough to feel vibrant, yet small enough to foster a sense of community.

My four years at George Fox were life-changing. I learned from brilliant faculty who were both experts in their fields and passionate about their faith. I met students from varying backgrounds within Christianity, encountering different denominational and theological commitments. It was a time of self-reflection and growth, learning more of what I believed and why I believed it. My faith is stronger for the time I spent as a student in Christian higher education, experiencing how faith and learning should not be compartmentalized but instead work as complementary pillars of a fully realized Christian life. Indeed, it was here where I first discerned my calling to teach college students in this environment, leading me to my current position at John Brown University.

Both George Fox and John Brown are members of the Council for Christian Colleges and Universities (CCCU). In addition to providing a community for faculty, staff, and administrators at these institutions, the CCCU advocates for the value of Christian higher education. Part of this, according to the CCCU's Shirley Hoogstra, means taking a step back from the so-called culture wars that threaten to hold Christians hostage to the concerns of the world. "I think that for us as leaders in Christian higher education," she said in an interview, "there has to be a conviction that we will not take on that mindset of siege.... The Creator God is not so fragile that he cannot take care of anything for which we would be under siege." Hoogstra later said that while there are certainly moments for Christians to be responsive and proactive to the issues of our day, we should not forget that God forever remains sovereign on his heavenly throne.

Christian higher education means more than starting classes with prayer or requiring students to attend chapel services once or twice a week. Instead, it is a holistic model of education preparing students not just for their future jobs but for living as Christians in a non-Christian world. It is a form of intellectual and spiritual discipleship, encouraging students to make connections between myriad fields and disciplines and the timeless truths of the Christian faith. Christian higher education acknowledges that all truth is God's truth, that there is not, as Abraham Kuyper wrote, "one square inch" that does belong to Jesus. Indeed, given Jesus's words in Matthew 22, the work of Christian higher education is in some sense inevitable: "Christians will always be in the education business," wrote historian Thomas Kidd, "as we seek to love God with all of our minds."[19]

Nevertheless, Christian higher education is in the process of confronting existential threats, driven largely by the same sorts of challenges described in chapter 3. In addition to a cultural environment where Christian universities may be viewed with increasing suspicion, the more pernicious and serious threat is demographic. Declining birth rates—made worse by

---

19. Kidd, "Coming Storm for Christian Higher Education."

the Great Recession—means there are going to be fewer and fewer college-aged Americans in the years ahead. With so many Christian colleges and universities dependent on revenue from tuition to meet their yearly expenses, the loss of just a few students per year could spur major changes in how these institutions operate.[20] The country's most elite universities can survive on billion-dollar endowments; most Christian colleges simply do not have this cushion on which to fall back. Only a handful of Christian colleges and universities maintain endowments of more than $100 million, and even these are not large enough to insulate their colleges from inevitable pressures.

At the very least, these pressures will require cutbacks[21]—and, in some cases, closures. In February 2023, Trinity International University announced it would be shuttering most of its physical campus and transitioning to online education, driven in large part by steadily declining enrollment in recent years.[22] And as of this writing, The King's College—a bastion for Christian liberal arts education in New York City—faces the prospect of collapse due to its financial woes.[23] Baylor's Matthew Lee Anderson observes a similar future for many Christian colleges and universities: "The great reconfiguration of Christian higher education is now underway," he wrote. "I am sorry for the upheaval this will bring to students and faculty."[24] If the coronavirus pandemic was a serious blow to the finances of too many in Christian higher education, then the looming demographic cliff may very well prove to be the knockout punch.

Aside from these broader demographic pressures are more specific challenges. For example, while women have generally outnumbered men at Christian colleges and universities, this gender gap has grown in recent years.[25] But women outnumbering men is not the problem—rather, it is that college-educated women report that they wouldn't consider a romantic relationship with someone who didn't go to college.[26] If fewer men at-

20. Speaking with *The Gospel Coalition*'s Colin Hansen, political science professor Ryan Burger didn't mince words: "That's why I don't teach at a Christian college, by the way, because five years of bad enrollments and your job's gone, because your university's gone." See Hansen and Burge, "Why Americans Quit Church."
21. Adams, "Hundreds of Positions Eliminated at Evangelical Colleges and Universities."
22. McClellan, "TIU Announces Plans to Move Undergrad Program Online."
23. Belz, "King's College Faces Threat of Closure."
24. Anderson, "Great Reconfiguration of Christian Higher Education."
25. McClellan, "Christian Colleges Look for 'Missing Men.'"
26. Cox, "College Dating Divide."

tend and graduate college, that narrows the pool of prospective spouses for women, particularly among evangelicals. And this will only exacerbate the demographic challenges for evangelicals in the years ahead, especially when combined with the rise of the "nones" in American religion and the subtle yet steady decline of church attendance and membership.

Then there's the larger problem of higher education increasingly being seen as transactional rather than transformational.[27] In this model students see themselves more as consumers and less as learners, seeking a degree not for the purpose of being formed as a thinker and a person but rather for the resulting economic benefits. Moreover, prospective students demand newer and better campus amenities to justify the cost of a college education; inevitably, an arms race plagues administrators desperate for any edge against competing institutions. This disordered educational marketplace is not unique to Christian institutions, but it arguably stands out more. "The market mind," writes Geneva College's Eric Miller, "is not the Christian mind."[28]

Still, amid these serious challenges for Christian higher education are emerging opportunities. Michael Lindsay has served as president of both Gordon College and Taylor University, major institutions of Christian higher education. He told me that while the landscape of Christian higher education will no doubt change in the years ahead, these colleges will play an increasingly important role in shaping and preparing young Christians:

> I see so many families questioning the value of paying tuition dollars to institutions that are actively working to undermine the moral formation they've dedicated eighteen years of their child's development toward, and so I think, as we see a rising tide of secularism in the academy, [this] creates a lot of great opportunity for us in the Christian sector.[29]

John Brown University's Chip Pollard is similarly optimistic, telling me Christian colleges and universities will stand out more in a post-Christian society than in generations past. "I think it's part of the Christian witness that we are actively present. . . . The church carries on. And Christian higher education should serve that, which is God's institution to carry out His ministry in this world."[30] While it would be naïve to believe that

27. Gehrz, "Pessimism for the Future of the Christian College."
28. Miller, "Market Made Me Do It."
29. Lindsay, personal interview.
30. Pollard, personal interview.

"the great reconfiguration" will somehow pass over Christian colleges and universities, the institutions that remain will be in a good position to serve students well as they prepare to serve God as leaders in their fields, communities, and the church.

In this spirit, Christian colleges and universities can prepare students to model a form of civic engagement different from (and better than) the world's. Notre Dame's Patrick Deneen told journalist Ezra Klein colleges should be doing more than giving students technical skills and training; instead, he said, colleges—and I'll suggest, *especially* Christian colleges—can be making positive arguments to students about the importance of investing in and building local communities. "It would be something that has a potentially profound effect," Deneen said, "for our students to become not merely what we regard as leaders in the national or international system, but as leaders in more local or regional kinds of communities."[31] In an era of increasing automation and skepticism around the value of higher education, our approach must be focused on how higher education can advance God's kingdom, not just prepare students for future careers.

In some circles—especially among political conservatives—it has become fashionable to disparage higher education as an increasingly irrelevant sector of society, focused more on creating and adopting the latest buzzwords than preparing students for meaningful lives in the decades following graduation. These critiques, while often exaggerated, are not entirely without merit. Yet the solution should not be to abandon higher education altogether. Yes, our country needs tradespeople and skilled laborers, for whom college education would be superfluous. But, as Peter Wood urges, we also need sharp and incisive thinkers, leaders who understand fundamental and foundational elements of the human condition, particularly as we encounter new technologies and related challenges. "America's ivory tower is collapsing," he writes, "and new ones need to be built."[32]

If it is true that colleges and universities have become caught up in the larger arms race for resources driven by pressures of enrollment—and many indications suggest that they have—then perhaps it is time for a reset.[33] Asbury University's Kevin Brown pleads for Christian universities to build spaces different—indeed, set apart—from the polarized and noxious environment too often prevalent in higher education. To be clear, Christian

---

31. Klein, "Transcript."
32. Wood, "Academia Needs Builders, Not Burners."
33. Smith, "Christian Universities Need a Reset."

colleges should not be cloistered, insular communities, turning inward while the world burns around them. Instead, these universities should offer markedly distinctive spaces for students to study the timeless truths of our world with the freedom and stability accompanying our identity in Christ. "Education," Brown writes, "is not about what we know; it is about what we love and who we *become*."[34]

Installing a liberal arts foundation for Christian higher education—regardless of discipline—is an appropriate place to focus such a reset. Writing for *Christianity Today*, Covenant College's Kelly Kapic reminds us that most Americans will have multiple jobs throughout their working years. Rather than preparing students for a relatively narrow understanding of work, Christian higher education can take a more ambitious tack:

> A Christian liberal arts education can prepare students not simply for a job, or even a career, but for vocation—the wisdom that hears God's call to respond with the whole self to produce meaning and purpose in God's world. Engaging a broad swath of learning in the concentrated context of Christian higher education can encourage a fair-minded, holistic approach to life, grounded on the Scriptures and the faith of the church through the ages.[35]

Kevin Brown continues, "We need liberal arts education so we do not unreflectively commit ourselves to the loudest voice or trendy ideas."[36] In that spirit, Christian higher education should not reflexively back away from difficult discussions, whether motivated by certainty or fear. Instead, committing to the liberal arts and pursuing the truth that accompanies these disciplines acknowledges our responsibility as being made in the image of God. "As a community of believers that desire to worship God with 'all of our minds,'" Brown writes, "we should never concede to dogmatic certainty that invites us to stop listening."[37] In an era of increasing polarization and division, this sort of reset is countercultural and potentially transformational—precisely what Christian higher education should be.

How can Christians strengthen the institutions best equipped to train and disciple the next generation of Christian leaders, artists, teachers, and citizens? How can we, to borrow language from my university, support institutions committed to educating for "head, heart, and hand"? Two things

---

34. Brown, "An Appeal from a Christian Liberal Arts University President."
35. Kapic, "Why We Still Need Christian Colleges."
36. Brown, "An Appeal from a Christian Liberal Arts University President."
37. Brown, "An Appeal from a Christian Liberal Arts University President."

come to mind. First, look beyond culture warring and political positioning to identify colleges and universities committed to the holistic development of their students. Plenty of colleges and universities have—strategically, it seems—placed a real value on positioning themselves as an ideological alternative to the status quo. And while crafting such an identity certainly appeals to some students and parents, it is not without its costs—namely, the temptation for the institution to see its very existence as dependent on the trench warfare of negative partisanship and social polarization.

I am not saying that *any* ideologically minded university has its priorities out of place. Grove City College, for example, is considered one of the preeminent conservative colleges in the country while generally avoiding involving itself in every contemporary political dispute. Its conservatism is rooted in something deeper than the partisanship of the moment. At the same time, the College of the Ozarks is also a strong conservative institution, yet regularly finds a way to react to the cultural issues of the day. One example is found in athletics, where the college has refused to compete against teams whose players kneel for the national anthem. "It's a shame sporting events are being used to communicate disrespect for this great country," its former president said in a release. "We will not be a part of this."[38] This posture may command an audience, but I question the long-term wisdom of making culture warring a central part of a college's identity.

Most Christian colleges and universities serve socially and politically conservative constituencies, yet these institutions are not engaged in knee-jerk culture warring. This is not cowardice or an aversion to conflict, but rather a missional strategy that picks battles carefully and with the heart of Christ. Yes, there is a time to fight; the CCCU regularly files *amicus curiae* briefs at the US Supreme Court on religious freedom issues. But when everything becomes the most important fight of our lives—when any cultural conflict becomes a last stand on which our very survival hinges—then nothing truly is. Young Christian men and women should be discipled to think wisely, critically, and faithfully, adopting a posture of boldness while rejecting the false machismo that so often dominates our political discourse. Christians agreeing with that premise should support and invest in colleges and universities that do the same.

Second, seek opportunities to engage and partner with the Christian colleges and universities in your communities. One of the most rewarding things I do in my position at John Brown University is hosting speakers on

---

38. Riley, "If You Kneel, the Game Is over, C of O Tells Opposing Teams."

our campus, usually on topics at the intersection of faith and public life. But it is always nerve-wracking to walk into the speaker's main event not knowing what kind of audience will be there. Some of our events have drawn crowds of two hundred people, while others have drawn twenty. I'm always especially interested in seeing who we can bring from the surrounding area to campus. Given the time, work, and resources that go into hosting these speakers, I'd much rather see more guests to campus than fewer.

This is where you come in. If you're reading this chapter and value the kinds of work happening across most of Christian higher education, show it not just with your financial support but also your attention to what your local Christian college is doing. Sign up for updates highlighting upcoming events at your area campus. Attend sporting events, plays, and other student activities. Learn from visiting experts, artists, and influential voices committed to the integration of faith, learning, and public life. Get comfortable with supporting and—assuming you honestly can—affirming the university's mission. Colleges and universities often speak of the "town and gown relationship," referring to higher education's connections with its community. The onus is (and should be) on the college to initiate these relationships, but as a Christian in that community, please reach back.

Additionally, you might have skills, connections, or other gifts beneficial to educating and training young Christians in your community. Do you work in an environment where students could intern, or are you looking to hire young professionals? Get connected to the college's career services office. Do you have experience in a field closely tied to an area of study at the college? Reach out to faculty teaching on subjects you're passionate and knowledgeable about, particularly if there are ways to encourage or support their work and their students' learning. You do not have to have studied at a Christian university or work at a Christian university to support the mission of a Christian university.

"Even if you never went to a Christian college or university," writes author and English professor Alan Noble, "you are currently benefiting from the work of these institutions." Continuing, Noble summarized the essential work of Christian higher education in an increasingly post-Christian culture: "Even if a Christian college isn't your alma mater, it is *your* school; they are *our* schools. At their best, they serve the church. And the sooner we accept our shared responsibility, the sooner we can do the necessary work of shoring up the ruins."[39]

---

39. Noble, "Christian Colleges Are in Crisis."

Our world and culture may be changing, but that doesn't mean Christians must sit idly by and observe with helplessness. We can build and prepare. Investing in and partnering with Christian higher education are among the most constructive things we can do for the sake of God's kingdom in our current moment.

COMMITTING TO UNITY

As I outlined in chapter 2, polarization has divided most aspects of American society. Politics may be the most evident arena for polarization, but we see it virtually everywhere we look—what we watch, where we shop, where we live, and yes, where we worship. Some have described this cultural divide as pitting "elite evangelicals" against "Cracker Barrel Christians."[40] Of greater concern than restaurants, though, are our churches. In 1960 Martin Luther King Jr. famously said, "I think it is one of the tragedies of our nation . . . that 11 o'clock on Sunday morning is one of the most segregated hours, if not the most segregated hour, in Christian America." And while Dr. King was referring to racial divisions in the church several decades ago, it is nevertheless true that today's Christian community is no less polarized.

Sociologists have consistently identified the ways in which our houses of worship are increasingly divided in various ways, in terms of race, socioeconomics, and yes, politics. Polarization among Christians is not a distinctly American phenomenon, of course; divisions have haunted the church since its earliest days.[41] But as the United States continues its transition into a post-Christian culture, temptations for division and conflict in the American church will be increasingly strong. Research shows that Christians are looking at those among us holding opposing political views with skepticism at best, and derision at worst.

Writing for the website *Mere Orthodoxy*, Michael Graham and Skyler Flowers argue that American evangelicalism has fractured into six categories, ranging from conservative culture warriors to the deconstructed and even disaffiliated.[42] Most interestingly, they present a growing divide between evangelicalism's most ardent conservatives (the "Neo-Fundamentalist Evangelicals") and more moderate yet theologically orthodox believers (the "Neo-Evangelicals"). The former is critical of what they see as the latter's

---

40. Wolfe, "Cracker Barrel Christians vs. Elite Evangelicals."
41. For two examples, see Acts 15:36–41 and Galatians 2:11–14.
42. Graham and Flowers, "Six Way Fracturing of Evangelicalism."

capitulation in the culture wars, alleging the latter is currying favor with secular elites. The latter, on the other hand, is highly critical of the former's fusion of evangelicalism with contemporary Republican (and increasingly Trumpian) politics, arguing such a relationship poses irreparable harm to Christianity's public witness to an increasingly skeptical and complex world. This divide isn't believers versus nonbelievers. It is Megan Basham versus David French, *American Reformer* versus *Christianity Today*.

Ours is, of course, not the first moment in the history of Christianity ravaged by divisions within the church; after all, we haven't even started an *actual* war yet. But as we commit to investing in and strengthening our churches and colleges, so too should Christians commit to unity in the body of Christ. Our disagreements on political and cultural issues should not define our relationships with our brothers and sisters in Christ. "Our identity as the people of God is not rooted in being better than our ideological enemy in a culture war," wrote pastor and author Gavin Ortlund. "It is rooted in the gospel, the evangel, the message of God's grace in Jesus Christ."[43] When we forget this, we deplatform the most important element of who we truly are.

Consider the words of Psalm 133, which begins, "How good and pleasant it is when brothers dwell in unity!"[44] The author is not singing of *political* unity but rather unity of a much deeper and more transformational sort. The psalmist here refers to unity among the tribes of Israel, unity that bridged their differences—if temporarily—under the reign of King David. A cohesive and united Israel was pleasing to God and nourishing to God's people, much like anointing oil and refreshing dew in the desert. Christians today can look to this psalm for advice in our fellowship, seeking to dwell together despite our differences under the banner of our risen savior. It is not naïve or lofty to think that Christians affirming the essentials of the faith can do this. Indeed, if we take the Bible seriously, this must be our aim.

But what does this sort of unity look like in practice? Consider two suggestions. First, reject the temptation to ascribe the worst motives to those with whom we disagree. Critics of so-called "evangelical elites" might be tempted to assume people like Tim Keller and Russell Moore are driven by a desire to maintain status with secular gatekeepers. At the same time, those critical of Christians voting for Donald Trump may be tempted to believe they are driven by xenophobia, misogyny, and idolatrous Christian

---

43. Ortlund, "Evangelical Self-Criticism."
44. Psalm 133:1.

nationalism. There are undoubtedly those in both communities who have dubious motives for their behaviors; we are, after all, fallen people. But Christians should not automatically apply these motives to their perceived opponents. We should let charity and grace drive our initial impressions of our fellow Christians, particularly on contested political and cultural issues.

I'll share a personal example. During one of President Biden's recent addresses to Congress, I was scrolling through the website formerly known as Twitter when I noticed a picture of Rep. Marjorie Taylor Greene shouting at Biden from her seat in the House chamber. I do not know the substance of her complaints, but her appearance that evening—she was dressed in a white fur sweater—reminded me of the White Witch from C. S. Lewis's *The Lion, the Witch, and the Wardrobe*. Naturally, I wanted to share my thoughts with the world, so I tweeted a picture of her next to a picture of the president, along with Aslan's famous quote from Lewis's classic story: "Do not cite the Deep Magic to me, Witch. I was there when it was written."

Most of the people who reacted seemed to share my amusement, but some thought the tweet was inappropriate, mainly due to my seemingly equating Biden with the Christ-figure of Aslan.[45] But one response from a relatively influential conservative Christian caught me completely off guard. He suggested I was calling Rep. Taylor Greene an *actual witch* and wrote that I would have never made a similar comment about a Democratic congresswoman. He then called on me to delete such an offensive and un-Christlike tweet. I responded by explaining my thought process about the joke, before saying I absolutely would have made a similar joke if the political parties were reversed (which, I can assure you, I would have). He told me, in no uncertain terms, that he did not believe me, and again called me to delete my supposedly hateful tweet. Clearly, we were at an impasse.[46]

In reflecting on this exchange, I was offended that someone I had never met was so confident about impugning my motives that he would tell me so to my (digital) face. Of course, I'm sure I've done the same to people countless times away from the public eye of social media. The driver whose indecisiveness at the intersection was obviously indicative of selfishness and poor skills at the wheel. My fellow church member whose objectionable political opinion was the result of ignorance and spiritual immaturity.

---

45. This certainly wasn't the point I was making, although I can see how some people may have thought so. The lesson, as always, is, "Never tweet."

46. I didn't delete the tweet; it was a silly joke, and the rare kind that allowed me to reference my interests in both American politics and C. S. Lewis.

As Christians, we must guard against these tendencies. Being charitable to those with whom we disagree is not just an important part of citizenship; it is an essential part of Christian formation. "Forgive us our debts," Jesus taught us to pray, "as we also have forgiven our debtors."[47]

As for a second suggestion, embrace humility when interacting with others, especially other Christians. In chapter 4 I wrote that humility is essential to a better Christian political engagement and posture. Certainty in politics is a dangerous thing, particularly when there are multiple vantage points from which to approach a complicated issue. But in the context of Christian unity, humility means being willing to accept that there may be real problems coming from your community—and acknowledging this is not only okay, but also a testament to God's forgiveness, grace, and mercy amid sin and fallenness.

American evangelicalism has seen its share of internal challenges in recent years, from tepid—or, in some instances, nonexistent—responses to cases of abuse to disagreements over how to respond to calls for racial justice. While *Mere Orthodoxy*'s Neo-Evangelicals tend to emphasize the need for repentance and accountability in certain congregations and denominations, Neo-Fundamentalist Evangelicals generally downplay these challenges as overblown—and potentially politically motivated. The *real* threat, they argue, is not coming from inside our own house but rather from outside forces seeking to sow division in the church. The challenges I described in chapter 3 are real—shouldn't we, these Christians ask, be more focused on *them*?

Dan Darling is an author, pastor, and leader concerned about the health of Christian communities. Importantly, Darling acknowledges that threats to the vitality of Christian spaces can come from both inward *and* outward sources.[48] "If we lament the waywardness of the culture more than we lament the misconduct of the church," he writes, "we are indeed getting our priorities exactly wrong." At the same time, though, Darling recognizes the importance of being on guard against encroaching cultural pressures, especially when such pressures threaten the legitimacy and holiness of the church. "Sometimes," he writes, "the purity of the church is compromised by accommodation to cultural pressures without." People (Christians among them) are drawn to simple "us versus them" models of the world. Embracing humility in the service of Christian unity rejects simplicity for

---

47. Matthew 6:12.
48. Darling, "In Here, Out There."

nuance, holding our preferred narratives loosely and considering uncomfortable alternatives.

To be sure, striving for and committing to unity does not mean refusing to engage in important debates and discussions over areas of disagreement and contention. Unity is not unanimity or homogeneity. It is not "niceness." Christians can and *should* disagree with one another on matters of paramount importance, particularly when it comes to how we best love our neighbors through politics and self-governance. But we must do this in a faithful posture and generous spirit, committing to maintain a united front and confident witness to a world in deep, deep need of the good news of Jesus.

FORMING AND FORMED

Human beings are social creatures by nature. We are born into communities, build families, and create associations and institutions to serve our common interests. But just as we form institutions, these same institutions also end up forming us. Churches and Christian education are critical modes of holistic Christian formation, ideally sharpening and sanctifying us every hour of the week and beyond the limited confines of the classroom. Similarly, striving for unity in the body of Christ—and, by extension, refusing to let important but ultimately secondary differences divide us—shapes our habits and character, reminding us not only of our own limitations but also of the beauty in the diversity of the people of God.

While our institutions form us, they also shape our collective culture, politics, and society. The spaces we cultivate and comprise play an essential role in influencing our communities. For Christians, this means the chance to reinvest in our institutions for the sake of a new kind of engagement, one that comes from an increasingly minoritarian and even marginalized perspective. In the afterword to Michael Bird's *Religious Freedom in a Secular Age*, theologian Bruce Ashford wrote, "Our churches, seminaries, and educational institutions must work together to reemphasize the public nature of Christianity."[49] For too long Christians—especially white evangelicals—in the United States have emphasized the private nature of Christianity, focusing on personal conversion and sanctification, while essentially downplaying the implications of personal faith for public life. But personal faith, if real, will inevitably have consequences for our shared life

49. Bird, *Religious Freedom in a Secular Age*, 173.

together. In investing in institutions and committing to Christian unity, we can take an important step toward that realization.

Despite the promise of trials in the years ahead, cultural retreat is not an option for Christians. While we should step back and consider how we're ordering our priorities, our world needs the hope of Christ through our public witness. Consider this from Patrick Schreiner: "We don't run and build Christian communes; we stay. We know our life is of no value in itself, we remain to testify. The fire of heaven will come from our mouths. Ironically, the boats leaving the city might be the very ones that shipwreck our faith."[50] Instead, Christians ought to invest in engagement, finding new ways to reach a changing culture with the truth of the gospel. "Evangelical witness matters," wrote Samuel James for *The Gospel Coalition*. "Does it matter enough to us?"[51] We have the opportunity to answer resoundingly in the affirmative in the years and decades ahead. The time to build and invest in institutions is now.

Let's get to work.

---

50. Schreiner, *Political Gospel*, 187.
51. James, "How to Renew a Decadent Evangelical Culture."

7

Comfort in the Uncomfortable

"And the things of earth will grow strangely dim."[1]

Earlier in this book I confessed that I don't like politics all that much. I would never describe myself as political junkie. I can't stand the back-and-forth exchanges on cable news and Sunday morning talk shows. And as a political science professor, I usually keep my own political beliefs and opinions close. The last thing I want to do is communicate to my students that if they don't share my views then they're at a disadvantage in my classes. Instead, I want to teach critical thinking and analysis. I want to equip my students to identify and make good use of evidence. I want to help them learn to make grounded arguments. I fail to see how advertising my political views helps me in these goals.

To be clear, I don't judge my colleagues who are more forthcoming about their political views in the courses they teach, assuming they aren't shaming or grading down students who disagree with them.[2] But my method has generally worked well for me. Sometimes, though, I forget to take off my professor's hat when leaving campus. On more than one occasion my wife and I have had a conversation like this:

---

1. From "Turn Your Eyes Upon Jesus" (1922), by Helen Howarth Lemmel.
2. Princeton's Robert George is an excellent example of this kind of professor, one who is unabashedly open about his conservatism yet whose students from across the political spectrum rave about his instruction and guidance.

Did you read about what that congressman said?
Yeah, I saw that.
What do you think about it?
Well, I get the motivation, but I can also see how people might be troubled by it.
Okay, but what do you *think?*
It's a tough one, for sure. The rhetoric seems strategically motivated to get his supporters fired up, especially as the primary election gets closer. But it could backfire with swing voters, and I'm definitely concerned about the larger message it sends.
Alright. How about the policy he was talking about?
It's all about trade-offs, I think. What do we value? What do we prioritize? I can see both sides.
You're insufferable.

Okay, so she hasn't ever *directly* called me insufferable, but I can tell she's thought it on more than one occasion. And after reflecting on these conversations over the years, I don't blame her. It's important to be able to take a stand on important issues of the day, especially on issues that directly implicate the Christian faith.[3] Striving for objectivity and to be above the political fray can easily lead to disengagement.

In this book I have tried to show why political disengagement is not a viable option for Christians. It is tempting at times to turn away from the challenges and discomfort of contemporary politics and all it entails, but discomfort is not a license to ignore. Our role as citizens of two kingdoms may be difficult, but it is not negotiable. Christians are clearly called to be in the world while remaining apart from the world. This is decidedly not an invitation to passivity or seclusion; it is a requirement to the sort of engagement I have described in previous chapters.

In this final chapter I address a few of the questions I've seen Christians ask about the relationship between faith and politics. Some of these questions involve practical matters, like voting and party identification. Some of them are more fundamental to our systems and philosophy of government. But they all show a desire to engage with some of the most important questions of the day. The least I can do, as a political science professor, an American, and a Christian, is attempt to provide some answers.[4]

---

3. Disputes over abortion and immigration have clearer and more obvious connections to Christianity than, say, debates over marginal tax rates and funding for public broadcasting.

4. In his book *A New Kind of Conservative*, Pastor Joel Hunter structures his final chapter in the same way I do here. I learned this after I started writing this chapter,

LET'S GET RIGHT DOWN TO IT: CAN SOMEONE VOTE FOR A DEMOCRAT AND STILL BE A FAITHFUL CHRISTIAN?

Yes, just as someone can vote for a Republican and still be a faithful Christian. Our political system usually gives us two imperfect choices on the ballot, and I think it's a mistake to claim that one of these choices will always be out of bounds for Christians. Both the Democratic Party's and Republican Party's platforms include elements that could appeal to many Christians. For Democrats, it could be an expanded social welfare system and a reformed immigration system more welcoming to people from troubled regions. For Republicans, it could be supporting restrictions on abortion and situating government power at local rather than national levels.

Of course, most white evangelical Christians—a group with which I identify—vote for Republican candidates. Given the party's position on abortion along with its traditionalism on gender and sexual politics, I think there are justifiable reasons for this. Also, as the Democratic Party has moved further to the left on these same issues—it wasn't that long ago that President Clinton called for abortions to be "safe, legal, and rare,"[5] and that President Obama voiced his opposition to same-sex marriage[6]—white evangelicals may feel increasingly as if they have no other option.

Still, it's wrong to say that no Christian could possibly vote for a Democrat without betraying their faith convictions. What are we to say to the broad swath of our Black brothers and sisters who routinely vote for Democrats? For Black Protestants, voting for Democratic candidates is usually not about the party's support for abortion, but rather the party's support for civil rights and social programs more popular among Black Americans than their white counterparts.

Voting is rarely a simple process without distinctions or qualifications; individual candidates contain multitudes, and any one of our political parties attracting these candidates are too broad to encompass *every* "Christian" policy position. Acknowledging that Christians can vote differently without betraying their faith is merely a recognition of the difficulty of voting in complex political systems.

---

but I'm sticking with this format. Great minds—and, in this case, my mind and Pastor Hunter's—think alike, it seems. See Hunter, *New Kind of Conservative*.

5. Flanagan, "Losing the 'Rare' in 'Safe, Legal, and Rare.'"
6. Steinmetz, "See Obama's 20-Year Evolution on LGBT Rights."

BUT SURELY THERE ARE SOME CANDIDATES WORTHIER OF A CHRISTIAN'S VOTE THAN OTHERS, RIGHT?

I certainly think so. There are some candidates I could never bring myself to vote for, for a variety of reasons. For example, I will never vote for Donald Trump, and would have a difficult time voting for anybody who has praised and defended the most damaging aspects of his presidency. At the same time, I could never bring myself to vote for Joe Biden, given his rhetoric on and support for abortion rights and antagonism toward the religious freedom claims of people in my community. Even though I can find things to value about both of their presidencies, for me, Trump and Biden will never be worthy of my vote. For me, there are always better options.

This is where I think it's important to listen to Christians who arrive at different political conclusions than ours. We ought to consider the motivation or driving force behind these votes. Is voting for a candidate a means to an end of certain policy priorities, or a way of signaling disdain and derision toward your political opponents? I may think a candidate is wholly undeserving of my vote as a Christian, whereas the person sitting in the pew next to me may have arrived at a fundamentally different conclusion. I may disagree with that outcome, just as he may disagree with mine. But we need not consider the other an apostate as a result.

WOULD IT BE BETTER FOR CHRISTIANS TO VOTE FOR THIRD-PARTY CANDIDATES? SHOULD CHRISTIANS REJECT THE TWO MAJOR PARTIES ALTOGETHER?

This is one strategy, for sure. It's how I voted for president in both 2016 and 2020, given the choices offered from both major parties.[7] But I hesitate to make such a definitive statement about the superiority of minor parties in *all* cases. It's possible that future Republican and Democratic candidates will win me over enough to earn my vote. There are Republicans today I would almost certainly support in the future, just as there are some Democrats for whom I would consider voting.

---

7. At the same time, I have the benefit (or curse) of voting in a state where the outcome for presidential elections is essentially predetermined. If I lived somewhere with a more competitive contest, perhaps I'd consider this choice differently.

Instead of committing to support one party—or neither party—election after election, Christians would be wise to approach every election with humility and openness about the choices before them. Partisanship can be a useful heuristic, signaling what kind of candidates we can usually expect to support. But party identification is not a perfect substitute for examining our options on a case-by-case basis.

As for the second question, this is a matter of personal judgment. I think it's a problem that Christians have not been more willing to use our influence in the Republican Party to demand more from our leaders there, in terms of character and electoral behavior. I also think it's a shame that Democrats have effectively purged pro-life voices from the party, creating an environment where many Christians otherwise open to Democratic priorities do not feel welcomed or valued.

There is something to be said for seeking to reform and reshape institutions rather than abandoning them altogether. Justin Giboney is not shy about his Democratic affiliation, even though his pro-life views place outside the mainstream of the party.[8] And governors like Arkansas's Asa Hutchinson have bucked the prevailing Trumpist influence in Republican Party politics while remaining committed to conservative policymaking and small government.[9] I wish more Christians—and, for the record, I'm including myself here—would be willing to do this work instead of either falling in line or walking away.

DO YOU THINK IT'S OKAY FOR CHRISTIANS TO NOT VOTE AT ALL?

Not voting can be about sending a message, just as voting can be. If you truly can't find anything to support in any of the candidates running for office, then abstaining is a reasonable course to take. That said, in any election there usually quite a few candidates and issues on the ballot, including at the state and local levels. While it's reasonable to abstain from voting in some races, sitting out the election entirely (and therefore ignoring the other elements of one's ballot) is less defensible.

But given that voting is the clearest way for citizens—and Christians—to make their political voices heard, remaining silent as a default could easily give way to indifference. And political indifference is something

---

8. Jones, "Lonely but Determined, pro-Life Democrats Speak Up."
9. Cillizza, "This Republican Governor Wants to Move on from Donald Trump."

Christians, called to be the hands and feet of Jesus, should actively reject. Put differently, Christians deciding *not* to vote should put as much prayer and discernment into that choice as they do when determining *how* to vote.

IS IT OKAY FOR CHRISTIANS TO BE A SINGLE-ISSUE VOTERS?

Christians can have different answers to this question without losing their faith. For some Christians—including many evangelicals and Catholics—the issue of abortion will always be of paramount importance in deciding how to vote. I certainly understand this approach, given the stakes for the unborn in our midst. I wouldn't fault any Christian who makes a candidate's opposition to abortion *the* factor in his or her vote choice. I also wouldn't fault any Christian who takes a more holistic approach to their political decision-making, weighing a variety of a candidate's views against his or her opponent's, and voting accordingly.

For me, an issue of paramount importance is support for constitutional principles. I want a candidate to affirm the rule of law and the supremacy of constitutional law over shifting political considerations. I want a candidate to respect the results of free and fair elections, rejecting the opportunism that comes with questioning the validity of a lost election. I find it hard to imagine voting for any candidate who takes steps to erode the legitimacy of our constitutional system of government. And while I would passionately argue that all Christians should be equally zealous of these principles, I wouldn't doubt the faith of a Christian solely because she doesn't share my enthusiasm for these things.

OKAY, SO HOW DO I PRIORITIZE THE ISSUES THAT DETERMINE WHO I SHOULD VOTE FOR?

I'm sorry, but this a decision only you can make. I will say, though, that I'm confident that there isn't a right or wrong answer. If you asked ten people you consider to be wise and mature Christians to rank their ten most important political issues, I'm willing to bet you'd get ten different lists—many of the issues in their lists would likely be the same, but the rankings would almost certainly be different from person to person.

Prioritizing political issues as a way of informing voting behavior comes down to what you value most in the political process. Your reading of Scripture and prayerful discernment ought to color your vision for a good and flourishing society, which should in turn inform the issues you find most important as you cast your ballot. Most Christians probably wouldn't consider tax rates on investment earnings the most important issue in their political calculus. Other issues, such as those relating to abortion or welcoming and supporting refugees, would probably resonate more deeply.

It is in keeping with a theme of this book that faithful Christians can disagree about the primacy of political issues as an influence on our political decision-making. Just because you don't share the same ranking of important issues as your Christian neighbors doesn't make you (or them) any less worthy of your identity in Christ. Ideally, Christians should recognize that life, immigration, education, civil rights and liberties, and other things are important to our political calculations. How we order these things is a matter of personal conviction and calling.

I'VE HEARD A LOT ABOUT "CHRISTIAN NATIONALISM." WHAT EXACTLY IS WRONG WITH CHRISTIANS SUPPORTING A DISTINCTLY CHRISTIAN GOVERNMENT?

There isn't anything wrong with Christians wanting government to pursue the common good and the flourishing of its people. After all, everybody bases their vision for good government and public policy on foundational conceptions of the good life. One need not be a Christian (or even religious) to have their political views influenced by deeply held beliefs. In the words of David Foster Wallace, "Everybody worships."[10] By itself, a Christian wanting government to make policy consistent with Christian values is not out of step with the norms of pluralistic democracy.

Christian nationalism is different. In chapter 5 I explained how the term is contested by academics and activists. Still, at a basic level, Christian nationalists might argue for establishing an overtly Christian government, giving preference to Christianity over other religious traditions, criminalizing sins like blasphemy, and the like. Christian nationalism is not a desire to see more Christians in elected office, nor is it a belief that our country

---

10. See Wilkinson, "Everybody Worships."

would be better off by adhering to Christian principles. Christian nationalism is using the levers and mechanisms of government to privilege Christians at the expense of non-Christians.

As an idea, Christian nationalism might seem appealing to those of us who believe in the truth of the Bible and the supremacy and sovereignty of God. Wouldn't it be good, we might ask, to use the power of the state to enforce what we know to be the best life on its citizens? We should remember, though, that nobody can come to Jesus through coercion or force. Similarly, Christians cannot confuse apparent political and cultural dominance with a healthy and vibrant faith. We must remember that Jesus did not promise his disciples political power, but rather subjugation at the hands of earthly authorities; their reward would come later, just as ours will.

Still, this does not mean Christians should refrain from using our faith to inform and justify our political decisions. People's political preferences are formed by myriad influences and experiences, including religious convictions. A Christian cannot be expected to separate his faith from his politics any more than a Muslim, a woman, an immigrant, a Black person, or a poor person should be expected to separate major aspects of his identity from his politics. It is a blessing of pluralism to have so many voices influencing our political conversations. Christians leaning on their faith in the public square is just one of example.

BUT IF GOD'S TRUTH IS THE ONLY TRUTH, THEN WHY SHOULDN'T I FIGHT FOR CHRISTIAN POLICIES OVER EVERYTHING ELSE?

This reminds me of an exchange I had with a speaker on my university's campus. He is an advocate of abortion abolition, meaning he does not support any instance of legal abortion, including when the health or life of the woman carrying the child is in jeopardy. To the abolitionist, abortion is nothing short of murder, and therefore should be not permitted in any circumstance. Abolitionists generally consider the mainstream pro-life movement as too accommodating and conciliatory.

After his prepared remarks, I asked him whether he would support a political candidate who pledged to ban abortion altogether but also to suspend the Constitution, cancel future elections, and govern as an authoritarian. He said he hadn't considered that question before, and would need to give it some thought. I wasn't surprised by his answer; for the abolitionist understanding abortion as murder and evil of the highest order, it's reasonable to consider whether preventing such evil would justify unsavory political means, even abandoning constitutional government altogether.

Here is where I stand: there is a major difference between advocating and fighting for Christian principles within the boundaries of a constitutional system, and imposing these principles while demolishing these constitutional boundaries. Christians should passionately commit themselves to the former while strongly rebuking the latter. Being made in the image of God affords people certain natural rights and autonomy, including the ability to choose their conception of the good life and the political regime most consistent with it. And the ability to determine one's political destiny is among the most fundamental rights a person has.

Christians should zealously advocate for justice on behalf of our neighbors and communities, but we should do so within the system that guarantees the rights we enjoy in the first place. Empowering the state to the degree Christian nationalism imagines may yield temporary victories for some Christians, but it is impossible to separate this power from the temptation—and I'd wager, inevitability—of despotism. Yes, Christians may not always win in constitutional democracies such as ours, but our hope is not found in favorable or even just political outcomes. Our hope lies beyond the broken and incomplete politics of this world.

IS THERE ANY REDEMPTION FOR THE TERM "EVANGELICAL" NOW THAT IT IS OFTEN EQUATED WITH A POLITICAL IDEOLOGY OR GROUP?

This question admittedly begs the question—namely, whether the term "evangelical" has been unhelpfully coopted by a particular political movement. I'm convinced "evangelical," as an identifier, has become increasingly associated with Republican Party politics in recent years. And I believe this is largely a negative development, inasmuch as it has confused what being an evangelical Christian really means. When politically conservative Muslims are declaring themselves to be evangelical, I think it's safe to say evangelical Christians have a marketing problem.[11]

At my university we have had more than a few conversations about whether it's useful to continue to identify as evangelicals, given the

---

11. Burge, "Why 'Evangelical' Is Becoming Another Word for 'Republican.'"

increasing political connotations of the label. I'm sympathetic to my colleagues who want no part of this conversation—not because they're not politically conservative, but because they don't want to malign other believers who don't share their political ideals. Then again, I'm not convinced it is time to abandon "evangelical" to the political world. After all, while the United States has the most evangelical Christians of any country on earth, more than 80 percent of the world's evangelicals live somewhere other than the United States.[12] What makes American evangelicals think we have sufficient ownership of the term to feel confident in abandoning it?

What, then, are American evangelicals to do? How can we redeem our label and discourage its political abuse? First, we can do politics better, focusing less on partisan victories and more on a holistic pursuit of justice that confounds our political reality. And second, we can critique and defy leaders across the political aisle trying to use the evangelical community as a means to an end. Despite a changing religious landscape, evangelical Christians remain an influential political group. We have a distinct and hopeful voice. We should use it to upset the political status quo rather than affirm its worst impulses.

IS THERE ANY HOPE FOR OUR POLITICAL SYSTEM AND PROCESSES TO EVER BE EFFECTIVE AGAIN?

Human beings are prone to recency bias, where we view our current moment as unique in the context of history. And to an extent, this is correct—our moment *is* unique, in that the things happening today have never happened before. But this is true for *any* moment in history; things are always changing from year to year, from decade to decade, from generation to generation. We can acknowledge the unique challenges of our political moment without thinking our moment is uniquely challenging or difficult.

Consider the first years of the American republic. The Constitution had been ratified and our institutions were in place, but the norms and precedents we count on today to guide and reign in these institutions were in flux. Our leaders were bound by laws, yes, but they were also tasked with developing the norms and behaviors we take for granted today. Or consider the buildup to and aftermath of the Civil War. Hundreds of thousands of

---

12. Earls, "3 in 5 Evangelicals Live in Asia or Africa."

Americans had died, and the regional tensions we still see today were inflamed and raw. Research shows that today's political climate is approaching this level of hostility, and yet there is no indication we are on the brink of a civil war.

The Great Depression. The civil rights movement. The countercultural movement in the 1960s. I could go on. Americans face our fair share of challenges today, but we are not the first generation to be reckoning with significant disruptions to the status quo. And through it all, our system of government and political process has survived. It hasn't always been easy, nor has it always emerged unchanged or unscathed. But the basic constitutional structures implemented nearly 250 years ago remain intact.

This doesn't mean there aren't dangers on the horizon. Democratic reforms have given people more ownership over our political systems,[13] but they have also made these systems more dependent on the whims of an increasingly polarized public. This, paired with a legislative redistricting process that insulates most of our representatives from real electoral competition, reduces incentives for elected officials to bridge differences with their political opponents. Instead of rewarding policy innovation and creativity, our political system is increasingly rewarding inaction and extremism.

At the same time, though, our political system and processes are still generally working as designed. Major bills are passed on a (mostly) bipartisan basis. Government shutdowns are rare. And while normal inefficiencies can be frustrating, our system was not designed to be efficient. It was designed to temper the passions of disparate factions, and to require compromise and cooperation necessary for government of, by, and for the people—the *whole* people. The American political experiment has never been an exercise in easy governance, but govern it has.

Few things have brought my youngest son as much as joy as Lin-Manuel Miranda's hit musical *Hamilton*. For months the soundtrack, combining hip-hop with American history to tell the story of the "ten-dollar founding father," was all he wanted to listen to. I didn't fault him; the songs are catchy, the lyrics rich, and the substance of inherent interest to me as a lifelong student of American government and politics. It was only after we overheard

---

13. Two of these reforms are the Seventeenth Amendment—providing for the direct election of US senators—and more democratic accountability over primary elections.

him singing to himself how Hamilton was "reliable with the ladies" that we decided a break was in order.

Writing in *Christianity Today*, Andrew Wilson explains how *Hamilton* paints an accurate picture of America's post-Christian culture.[14] For Hamilton and his contemporaries, religion—and especially Christianity—was always in the background, just as it is today. Secularization may be moving apace in our country, but that does not mean the disappearance of Christianity altogether. According to Wilson,

> Religion is firmly in the background while we are winning wars and making money, and even while we are making shady deals and having affairs. Although Christianity still shapes our history, ethics, architecture, and psychology, we rarely think about it when times are good.
>
> But when things fall apart—when we lose our children or our partners, when we face death ourselves, when we have done something unimaginable and need forgiveness and grace—we know where to find help.

While our culture is not necessarily *more* open to the gospel compared to previous generations, it is certainly not *less* open. Christianity has always been fighting against the current of whatever is popular, whatever is fashionable, whatever is easy. It has always been up to Christians to carry the good news faithfully, pointing to a different and better way. God is the potter; we are, in the best case, merely clay.

On any day it may seem as if we are at a particularly precarious political moment. As I wrote in earlier chapters, I certainly think there is evidence for this, from toxic political polarization and negative partisanship to seemingly inevitable demographic and cultural changes. Data complements anecdotes that our country is more divided than at any time since the Civil War. One might forgive Christians for pessimism or even fear about the future of our shared political experiment, and for adopting a political posture reflecting the apparent urgency of this moment.

But we have good reasons to reject such a posture. "What has been is what will be, and what has been done is what will be done," writes the author of Ecclesiastes, "and there is nothing new under the sun."[15] Our moment *is* challenging, but it is not unprecedented. American Christians are not the first to face difficulties on account of our faith, nor will we be the

14. Wilson, "It's Hamilton's World."
15. Ecclesiastes 1:9.

last. Tim Keller reminds us that today's Christians are not so different from the first generation of believers, in that the dominant political establishment has always accused Christians of not worshipping the right deities.[16] The only difference is *what* we are refusing to worship.

As Christians, our posture in response to the challenges of our time matter for God's kingdom just as much as political outcomes. We are a people called not to conquer our enemies by any means necessary, but to follow our savior's radical and countercultural example to the point of defeat, even to death. Yes, pursuing justice and the good of our neighbors is essential to our Christian witness; we must not eschew action for nihilism. But if the pursuit of justice is essential, so too is our ability to reckon with loss and move on faithfully, holding fast to the hope we have in our resurrected King and trusting that any earthly setback is not the end.

Christians are called to be comfortably uncomfortable with the tension of our dual citizenship, restoring politics to its rightful place as subordinate to our identity in Christ. At a moment and in a culture so intensely focused on politics as ultimate, our uneasy citizenship can be a balm for a wounded and hurting world. But first, we have to believe it ourselves.

---

16. Keller, "Roman Empire."

Bibliography

Abramowitz, Alan I., and Steven W. Webster. "Negative Partisanship: Why Americans Dislike Parties But Behave Like Rabid Partisans." *Advances in Political Psychology* 39 (2018) 119–35.

Abrams, Samuel J. "Polarization in American Family Life Is Overblown." *Survey Center on American Life*, February 23, 2022. https://www.americansurveycenter.org/polarization-in-american-family-life-is-overblown/.

Adams, Liam. "Hundreds of Positions Eliminated at Evangelical Colleges and Universities." *Christianity Today*, August 10, 2020. https://www.christianitytoday.com/news/2020/august/christian-college-cuts-bethel-harding-john-brown-cccu.html.

Ahmari, Sohrab. "Against David French-Ism." *First Things*, May 29, 2019. https://www.firstthings.com/web-exclusives/2019/05/against-david-french-ism.

Alba, Richard, Morris Levy, and Dowell Myers. "The Myth of a Majority-Minority America." *The Atlantic*, June 13, 2021. https://www.theatlantic.com/ideas/archive/2021/06/myth-majority-minority-america/619190/.

Alberta, Tim. "What the GOP Does to Its Own Dissenters." *The Atlantic*, December 7, 2021. https://www.theatlantic.com/magazine/archive/2022/01/peter-meijer-freshman-republican-impeach/620844/.

The American Conservative. "National Conservatism: A Statement Of Principles." *The American Conservative*, June 15, 2022. https://www.theamericanconservative.com/national-conservatism-a-statement-of-principles/.

Anderson, Matthew Lee. "The Great Reconfiguration of Christian Higher Education Is Now Underway. I Am Sorry for the Upheaval This Will Bring to Students and Faculty. Https://T.Co/99XFNfbrhU." *Twitter*, February 17, 2023. https://twitter.com/mattleeanderson/status/1626691135870586921.

Bailey, Sarah Pulliam. "Here's What We Know about the Faith of Sen. Cruz, Who's Set to Announce His 2016 Bid at Liberty University." *The Washington Post*, March 22, 2015. https://www.washingtonpost.com/news/acts-of-faith/wp/2015/03/22/heres-what-we-know-about-the-faith-of-sen-ted-cruz-whos-set-to-announce-his-2016-bid-at-liberty-university/.

Balkin, Jack. "The Not-So-Happy Anniversary of the Debt-Ceiling Crisis." *The Atlantic*, July 31, 2012. https://www.theatlantic.com/politics/archive/2012/07/the-not-so-happy-anniversary-of-the-debt-ceiling-crisis/260458/.

Balmer, Randall. "The Evangelical Abortion Myth: An Excerpt from 'Bad Faith.'" *Religion Dispatches*, August 30, 2021. https://religiondispatches.org/the-evangelical-abortion-myth-an-excerpt-from-bad-faith/.

Bibliography

———. "The Real Origins of the Religious Right." *Politico Magazine*, May 27, 2014. http://www.politico.com/magazine/story/2014/05/religious-right-real-origins-107133.html.

Banco, Erin. "In Alabama and Louisiana, Partisan Opposition to Vaccine Surges alongside Delta Variant." *Politico*, July 24, 2021. https://www.politico.com/news/2021/07/24/covid-vaccine-push-rural-500717.

Barton, David. *Original Intent: The Courts, the Constitution & Religion*. Aledo, TX: WallBuilder, 2000.

Beck, Howard. "Public Relations a Concern as N.B.A. Millionaires Spar." *The New York Times*, August 28, 2011. https://www.nytimes.com/2011/08/29/sports/basketball/nba-players-avoid-displays-of-luxury.html.

Belz, Emily. "The King's College Faces Threat of Closure." *Christianity Today*, February 28, 2023. https://www.christianitytoday.com/news/2023/february/kings-college-new-york-closure-financial-crisis.html.

Bennett, Daniel. "In Pluralism's Defense." *Law & Liberty*, December 14, 2022. https://lawliberty.org/in-pluralisms-defense/.

———. "LGBT Rights Ruling Isn't the Beginning of the End for Religious Liberty." *Christianity Today*, June 17, 2020. https://www.christianitytoday.com/ct/2020/june-web-only/bostock-gorsuch-supreme-court-ruling-religious-liberty.html.

———. "We Need to Be Better Losers." *Christianity Today*, January 6, 2021. https://www.christianitytoday.com/ct/2021/january-web-only/christian-victory-election-loss.html.

Berg, Matt. "Meijer: 'Not One' Regret over Trump Impeachment Vote despite Defeat." *Politico*, August 4, 2022. https://www.politico.com/news/2022/08/04/meijer-trump-impeachment-vote-defeat-00049843.

Bilbro, Jeffrey. *Reading the Times: A Literary and Theological Inquiry into the News*. Downers Grove, IL: IVP Academic, 2021.

Bird, Michael F. *Religious Freedom in a Secular Age: A Christian Case for Liberty, Equality, and Secular Government*. Grand Rapids: Zondervan, 2022.

Bishop, Bill. *The Big Sort: Why the Clustering of Like-Minded America Is Tearing Us Apart*. Boston: Mariner, 2009.

Blair, Leonardo. "Fewer than Half of American Adults Pray Daily; Religiously Unaffiliated Grows: Study." *The Christian Post*, December 17, 2021. https://www.christianpost.com/news/fewer-than-half-of-american-adults-pray-daily-study.html.

Blake, Nathanael. "For Americans To Have Freedom, They Must Revive The Common Good." *The Federalist*, June 5, 2019. https://thefederalist.com/2019/06/05/americans-freedom-must-revive-common-good/.

Blue, Alexis. "The Rise of Negative Partisanship and How It Drives Voters." University of Arizona, October 13, 2020. https://news.arizona.edu/story/rise-negative-partisanship-and-how-it-drives-voters.

Bob Jones University v. United States, 461 U.S. 574 (1983).

Bostock v. Clayton County, 590 U.S. 644 (2020).

Brody, David. "I Don't Know about You but I'll Take a President with a Bible in His Hand in Front of a Church over Far Left Violent Radicals Setting a Church on Fire Any Day of the Week. @POTUS @realDonaldTrump @WhiteHouse #StJohnsChurch Https://T.Co/84uZf6GAme." Twitter, June 2, 2020. https://twitter.com/DBrodyReports/status/1267646416689692672.

Bibliography

Brooks, David. "The Terrifying Future of the American Right." *The Atlantic*, November 18, 2021. https://www.theatlantic.com/ideas/archive/2021/11/scary-future-american-right-national-conservatism-conference/620746/.

Brown, Kevin. "An Appeal from a Christian Liberal Arts University President." *Mere Orthodoxy*, September 29, 2020. https://mereorthodoxy.com/appeal-christian-liberal-arts-university-president/.

Brown, Steven P. *Trumping Religion: The New Christian Right, the Free Speech Clause, and the Courts*. Tuscaloosa, AL: University of Alabama Press, 2002.

Burge, Ryan. "I Don't Think People Fully Grasp How Much of Protestant Christianity Is Going to Die off in the next 3 Decades." *Twitter*, February 1, 2023. https://twitter.com/ryanburge/status/1620913806003286019?s=46&t=j_1MMN7UYfEpVIUktUYNBQ.

———. *The Nones: Where They Came From, Who They Are, and Where They Are Going*. Minneapolis: Fortress, 2021.

———. "Rise of the 'nothing in Particulars' May Be Sign of a Disjointed, Disaffected and Lonely Future." *Religion News Service*, July 3, 2019. https://religionnews.com/2019/07/03/rise-of-the-nothing-in-particulars-may-be-sign-of-a-disjointed-disaffected-and-lonely-future/.

———. "Why 'Evangelical' Is Becoming Another Word for 'Republican.'" *The New York Times*, October 26, 2021. https://www.nytimes.com/2021/10/26/opinion/evangelical-republican.html.

Burnett, John. "Christian Nationalism Is Still Thriving—and Is a Force for Returning Trump to Power." *NPR*, January 23, 2022. https://www.npr.org/2022/01/14/1073215412/christian-nationalism-donald-trump.

Cai, Sophia. "Anti-Abortion Democrats Are a Dying Breed." *Axios*, May 27, 2022. https://www.axios.com/2022/05/27/abortion-democrats-supreme-court-midterms.

Carney, Timothy P. *Alienated America: Why Some Places Thrive While Others Collapse*. New York: Harper, 2019.

Carroll, Dave. "Church Is Messy." *Little Thoughts from Big Dave*, August 18, 2022. https://davecarroll.substack.com/p/church-is-messy.

Carter, Joe. "David Platt Prays for President Trump in Visit to McLean Bible Church." *The Gospel Coalition*, June 2, 2019. https://www.thegospelcoalition.org/article/david-platt-models-pray-president/.

Cassetto, Noah, Noelle Worley, and Helen Huiskes. "College to Reduce Faculty, Staff in Significant Budget Cuts." *The Wheaton Record*, November 18, 2022. https://thewheatonrecord.com/2022/11/17/college-to-reduce-faculty-staff-in-significant-budget-cuts/.

Castle, Jeremiah J., and Kyla K. Stepp. "Partisanship, Religion, and Issue Polarization in the United States: A Reassessment." *Political Behavior* 43 (2021) 1311–35.

Christianity Today. "The Rise and Fall of Mars Hill." https://www.christianitytoday.com/ct/podcasts/rise-and-fall-of-mars-hill/.

Cillizza, Chris. "This Republican Governor Wants to Move on from Donald Trump." *CNN*, May 2, 2022. https://www.cnn.com/2022/05/02/politics/asa-hutchinson-2024-plans-trump/index.html.

Colby, Sandra L., and Jennifer M. Ortman. "Projections of the Size and Composition of the U.S. Population: 2014 to 2060." *United States Census Bureau*, March 3, 2015. https://www.census.gov/library/publications/2015/demo/p25-1143.html.

Bibliography

Converse, Philip E. "The Nature of Belief Systems in Mass Publics (1964)." *Critical Review* 18 (2006) 1–74.

Conway, Madeline. "Spicer Claims That Jobs Numbers 'May Have Been Phony' before, but Now They're 'Very Real.'" *Politico*, March 10, 2017. https://www.politico.com/story/2017/03/trump-monthly-jobs-numbers-sean-spicer-235936.

Coppins, McKay. "The Christians Who Loved Trump's Stunt." *The Atlantic*, June 2, 2020. https://www.theatlantic.com/politics/archive/2020/06/trumps-biblical-spectacle-outside-st-johns-church/612529/.

Cosby, Brian. "Moralistic Therapeutic Deism: Not Just a Problem with Youth Ministry." *The Gospel Coalition*, April 9, 2012. https://www.thegospelcoalition.org/article/mtd-not-just-a-problem-with-youth-ministry/.

Cox, Daniel. "The College Dating Divide." *Institute for Family Studies*, February 20, 2023. https://ifstudies.org/blog/the-college-dating-divide.

———. "Generation Z and the Future of Faith in America." *Survey Center on American Life*, March 24, 2022. https://www.americansurveycenter.org/research/generation-z-future-of-faith/.

Cox, Daniel, and Amelia Thomson-DeVeaux. "Millennials Are Leaving Religion And Not Coming Back." *FiveThirtyEight*, December 12, 2019. https://fivethirtyeight.com/features/millennials-are-leaving-religion-and-not-coming-back/.

Darling, Dan. "In Here, Out There: On Assessing Spiritual Threats." *One Little Word*, April 18, 2021. https://dandarling.substack.com/p/in-here-out-there-on-assessing-spiritual.

Deneen, Patrick. "A Good That Is Common." *Postliberal Order*, November 8, 2021. https://postliberalorder.substack.com/p/a-good-that-is-common.

———. *Why Liberalism Failed*. New Haven: Yale University Press, 2018.

DeYoung, Kevin. "The Rise of Right-Wing Wokeism." *The Gospel Coalition*, November 28, 2022. https://www.thegospelcoalition.org/reviews/christian-nationalism-wolfe/.

Dimock, Michael, and Richard Wike. "America Is Exceptional in Its Political Divide." *Trust*, March 29, 2021. https://www.pewtrusts.org/en/trust/archive/winter-2021/america-is-exceptional-in-its-political-divide.

Djupe, Paul, and Jacob Neiheisel. "How Future Supreme Court Rulings May Fuel the Decline of Religion in the US." *Religion in Public*, July 15, 2022. https://religioninpublic.blog/2022/07/15/how-future-supreme-court-rulings-ruling-may-fuel-the-decline-of-religion-in-the-us/.

Dobbs v. Jackson Women's Health Organization, 597 U.S. ___ (2022).

Dred Scott v. Sandford, 60 U.S. 393 (1857).

Dreher, Rod. *The Benedict Option: A Strategy for Christians in a Post-Christian Nation*. New York: Sentinel, 2017.

———. *Live Not by Lies: A Manual for Christian Dissidents*. New York: Sentinel, 2020.

———. "Tucker To Hungary, Nixon To China." *The American Conservative*, August 4, 2021. https://www.theamericanconservative.com/dreher/tucker-to-hungary-nixon-to-china/.

Du Mez, Kristin Kobes. *Jesus and John Wayne: How White Evangelicals Corrupted a Faith and Fractured a Nation*. New York: Liveright, 2020.

Earls, Aaron. "3 in 5 Evangelicals Live in Asia or Africa." *Lifeway*, March 2, 2020. https://research.lifeway.com/2020/03/02/3-in-5-evangelicals-live-in-asia-or-africa/.

Bibliography

Edsall, Thomas B. "We Can't Even Agree on What Is Tearing Us Apart." *The New York Times*, May 25, 2022. https://www.nytimes.com/2022/05/25/opinion/polarization-politics-red-blue-america.html.

Eldredge, John. *Wild at Heart: Discovering the Secret of a Man's Soul.* Rev. and updated ed. Nashville: Thomas Nelson, 2011.

Emerson, Michael O., and Christian Smith. *Divided by Faith: Evangelical Religion and the Problem of Race in America.* New York: Oxford University Press, 2001.

The Enneagram Institute. "Type Nine." https://www.enneagraminstitute.com/type-9.

Esbeck, Carl. "Everything You Need to Know About the Respect for Marriage Act." *Christianity Today*, November 17, 2022. https://www.christianitytoday.com/ct/2022/november-web-only/same-sex-marriage-religious-liberty-respect-marriage-act.html.

Fea, John. *Believe Me: The Evangelical Road to Donald Trump.* Grand Rapids: Eerdmans, 2018.

Filkins, Dexter. "Can Ron DeSantis Displace Donald Trump as the G.O.P.'s Combatant-in-Chief?" *The New Yorker*, June 20, 2022. https://www.newyorker.com/magazine/2022/06/27/can-ron-desantis-displace-donald-trump-as-the-gops-combatant-in-chief.

Fiorina, Morris, Samuel Abrams, and Jeremy Pope. *Culture War? The Myth of a Polarized America.* Boston: Longman, 2010.

Flanagan, Caitlin. "Losing the 'Rare' in 'Safe, Legal, and Rare.'" *The Atlantic*, December 6, 2019. https://www.theatlantic.com/ideas/archive/2019/12/the-brilliance-of-safe-legal-and-rare/603151/.

Foust, Michael. "Trump Surprises Evangelical Church with Visit; Pastor Prays for Him." *ChristianHeadlines.com*, June 3, 2019. https://www.christianheadlines.com/contributors/michael-foust/trump-surprises-evangelical-church-with-visit-pastor-prays-for-him.html.

Fowler, Robert Booth, Allen D. Hertzke, Laura R. Olson, and Kevin R. Den Dulk. *Religion and Politics in America: Faith, Culture, and Strategic Choices.* 6th ed. New York: Westview, 2019.

French, David. "American Racism: We've Got So Very Far to Go." *The Dispatch*, June 7, 2020. https://thedispatch.com/newsletter/frenchpress/american-racism-weve-got-so-very/.

———. "A Christian Defense of American Classical Liberalism." *The Dispatch*, October 31, 2021. https://thedispatch.com/newsletter/frenchpress/a-christian-defense-of-american-classical/.

———. "The Complete Case for Kavanaugh." *National Review*, October 5, 2018. https://www.nationalreview.com/2018/10/kavanaugh-case-for-confirmation-allegations-explained/.

———. "A Critique of Tim Keller Reveals the Moral Devolution of the New Christian Right." *The Dispatch*, May 8, 2022. https://thedispatch.com/newsletter/frenchpress/a-critique-of-tim-keller-reveals/.

———. *Divided We Fall: America's Secession Threat and How to Restore Our Nation.* New York: St. Martin's, 2020.

———. "Punitive Intolerance Is No Way to Preserve Pluralism." *The Dispatch*, July 7, 2021. https://thedispatch.com/newsletter/frenchpress/punitive-intolerance-is-no-way-to/.

Friesen, Amanda, and Michael W. Wagner. "Beyond the 'Three Bs': How American Christians Approach Faith and Politics." *Politics and Religion* 5 (2012) 224–52.

Bibliography

Galston, William A. "Has Trump Caused White Evangelicals to Change Their Tune on Morality?" *Brookings Institution*, October 19, 2016. https://www.brookings.edu/blog/fixgov/2016/10/19/has-trump-caused-white-evangelicals-to-change-their-tune-on-morality/.

Gehrz, Chris. "Pessimism for the Future of the Christian College." *The Pietist Schoolman*, October 20, 2022. https://chrisgehrz.substack.com/p/pessimism-for-the-future-of-the-christian.

Gerson, Michael. "Prominent Evangelicals Are Directing Trump's Sinking Ship. That Feeds Doubts about Religion." *The Washington Post*, December 7, 2020. https://www.washingtonpost.com/opinions/prominent-evangelicals-are-directing-trumps-sinking-ship-that-feeds-doubts-about-religion/2020/12/07/5ad8eb0c-38c3-11eb-9276-ae0ca72729be_story.html.

———. "A Truly Sacrilegious Use of the Bible to Bless a Brutal Stunt." *Twitter*, June 1, 2020. https://twitter.com/MJGerson/status/1267595833001771010.

Giboney, Justin, Michael Wear, and Chris Butler. *Compassion (&) Conviction: The AND Campaign's Guide to Faithful Civic Engagement*. Downers Grove, IL: InterVarsity, 2020.

Goldberg, Michelle. "Leave Drag Queen Story Hour Alone!" *The New York Times*, June 7, 2019. https://www.nytimes.com/2019/06/07/opinion/conservatives-culture-trump.html.

Goodrich, Luke. *Free to Believe: The Battle Over Religious Liberty in America*. Colorado Springs: Multnomah, 2019.

Gorski, Philip S., and Samuel L. Perry. *The Flag and the Cross: White Christian Nationalism and the Threat to American Democracy*. New York: Oxford University Press, 2022.

Graham, Michael, and Skyler Flowers. "The Six Way Fracturing of Evangelicalism." *Mere Orthodoxy*, June 7, 2021. https://mereorthodoxy.com/six-way-fracturing-evangelicalism/.

Green, Lauren. "Critical Race Theory Debate Divides Christians: 'All of Us Have Intrinsic Value.'" *Fox News*, July 30, 2021. https://www.foxnews.com/politics/critical-race-theory-debate-divides-christians.

Green v. Connally, 330 F. Supp. 1150 (1971).

Greenhut, Steven. "Drag-Queen Debate Spotlights Creepy Trend on Right." *Orange County Register*, September 13, 2019. https://www.ocregister.com/drag-queen-debate-spotlights-creepy-trend-on-right.

Griswold, Kylee. "Instead Of Praising Roe's Death, Russell Moore Trashes Trump." *The Federalist*, July 29, 2022. https://thefederalist.com/2022/07/29/instead-of-praising-death-of-roe-v-wade-russell-moore-breaks-silence-to-trash-trump-and-his-voters/.

Gstalter, Morgan. "Franklin Graham Calls for 'Special Day of Prayer' to Protect Trump from Enemies." *The Hill*, May 28, 2019. https://thehill.com/homenews/administration/445699-franklin-graham-calls-for-special-day-of-prayer-to-protect-trump-from/.

Haberman, Clyde. "Religion and Right-Wing Politics: How Evangelicals Reshaped Elections." *The New York Times*, October 28, 2018. https://www.nytimes.com/2018/10/28/us/religion-politics-evangelicals.html.

Hagerty, Barbara Bradley. "The Most Influential Evangelist You've Never Heard Of." *NPR*, August 8, 2012. https://www.npr.org/2012/08/08/157754542/the-most-influential-evangelist-youve-never-heard-of.

Bibliography

Hall, Mark. *Did America Have a Christian Founding? Separating Modern Myth from Historical Truth*. Nashville: Thomas Nelson, 2019.

———. "Tilting at Windmills: The 'Threat' of Christian Nationalism." *Standing for Freedom Center*, February 8, 2022. https://www.standingforfreedom.com/2022/02/tilting-at-windmills-the-threat-of-christian-nationalism/.

Hammer, Josh. "Common Good Originalism." *The American Mind*, May 6, 2020. https://americanmind.org/features/waiting-for-charlemagne/common-good-originalism/.

———. "I Think @nytdavidbrooks Intended This to Be a Hit Piece, but He Inadvertently Found a Way to Make National Conservatism Sound Absolutely Awesome. Sign Me up! Https://Theatlantic.Com/Ideas/Archive/2021/11/Scary-Future-American-Right-National-Conservatism-Conference/620746/ Https://T.Co/LaZvKbUAAl." *Twitter*, November 18, 2021. https://twitter.com/josh_hammer/status/1461476293481013253.

Hanna, Alex, Nikki Stevens, Os Keyes, and Maliha Ahmed. "Actually, We Should Not All Use They/Them Pronouns." *Scientific American*, May 3, 2019. https://blogs.scientificamerican.com/voices/actually-we-should-not-all-use-they-them-pronouns/.

Hansen, Colin, and Ryan Burge. "Why Americans Quit Church." *The Gospel Coalition*, December 7, 2021. https://www.thegospelcoalition.org/podcasts/gospelbound/why-americans-quit-church/.

Hawkins, Matthew. "Why We Need the Church to Disciple Our Politics." *The Gospel Coalition*, March 23, 2021. https://www.thegospelcoalition.org/article/church-disciple-politics/.

Hochman, Nate. "What Comes After the Religious Right?" *The New York Times*, June 2, 2022. https://www.nytimes.com/2022/06/01/opinion/republicans-religion-conservatism.html.

Hoogstra, Shirley. Personal interview, October 25, 2021.

Huckabee, Tyler. "Sunday's Cool: Cave Exploring." *Clusterhuck*, March 5, 2023. https://tylerhuckabee.substack.com/p/sundays-cool-cave-exploring.

Hunter, Joel C. *A New Kind of Conservative*. Ventura, CA: Regal, 2008.

Inazu, John D. *Confident Pluralism: Surviving and Thriving through Deep Difference*. Chicago: University of Chicago Press, 2016.

Ingraham, Christopher. "19 Times Trump Called Jobs Numbers 'Fake' before They Made Him Look Good." *The Washington Post*, March 10, 2017. https://www.washingtonpost.com/news/wonk/wp/2017/03/10/19-times-trump-called-the-jobs-numbers-fake-before-they-made-him-look-good/.

Jacobs, Carly M., and Elizabeth Theis-Morse. "Belonging in a 'Christian Nation': The Explicit and Implicit Associations between Religion and National Group Membership." *Politics and Religion* 6 (2013) 373–401.

James, Samuel. "How to Renew a Decadent Evangelical Culture." *The Gospel Coalition*, April 20, 2022. https://www.thegospelcoalition.org/article/renew-decadent-evangelical-culture/.

———. "Is It Time to Move Past Tim Keller?" *Digital Liturgies*, May 8, 2022. https://samueldjames.substack.com/p/is-it-time-to-move-past-tim-keller.

James, Spencer, Hal Boyd, and Jason Carroll. "Why the Partisan Divide? The U.S. Is Becoming More Secular—and More Religious." *Religion and Politics*, November 17, 2020. https://religionandpolitics.org/2020/11/17/why-the-partisan-divide-the-u-s-is-becoming-more-secular-and-more-religious/.

Bibliography

Jenkins, Jack. *American Prophets: The Religious Roots of Progressive Politics and the Ongoing Fight for the Soul of the Country.* New York: HarperOne, 2020.

———. "Republicans Mostly Mum on Calls to Make GOP 'Party of Christian Nationalism.'" *The Washington Post,* August 19, 2022. https://www.washingtonpost.com/religion/2022/08/19/republicans-mostly-mum-calls-make-gop-party-christian-nationalism/.

———. "Scholars, Activists Brief Lawmakers on Role of Christian Nationalism at Insurrection." Religion News Service, March 18, 2022. https://religionnews.com/2022/03/18/scholars-activists-brief-lawmakers-on-role-of-christian-nationalism-at-insurrection/.

Jones, Jeffrey M. "U.S. Church Membership Falls Below Majority for First Time." *Gallup News,* March 29, 2021. https://news.gallup.com/poll/341963/church-membership-falls-below-majority-first-time.aspx.

Jones, Kevin. "Lonely but Determined, pro-Life Democrats Speak Up." *Catholic News Agency,* July 31, 2018. https://www.catholicnewsagency.com/news/39015/lonely-but-determined-pro-life-democrats-speak-up.

Jones, Robert P. *White Too Long: The Legacy of White Supremacy in American Christianity.* New York: Simon & Schuster, 2020.

Kaemingk, Matthew. "Making America Hospitable for Religious Outsiders." *Christianity Today,* February 18, 2019. https://christianitytoday.com/ct/2019/february-web-only/making-america-hospitable-for-religious-outsiders.html.

Kalmoe, Nathan P., and Lilliana Mason. *Radical American Partisanship: Mapping Violent Hostility, Its Causes, and the Consequences for Democracy.* Chicago Studies in American Politics. Chicago: University of Chicago Press, 2022.

Kapic, Kelly. "Why We Still Need Christian Colleges." *Christianity Today,* September 18, 2019. https://www.christianitytoday.com/ct/2019/october/kapic-we-need-christian-liberal-arts-colleges.html.

Keller, Tim. "How Do Christians Fit Into the Two-Party System? They Don't." *The New York Times,* September 29, 2018. https://www.nytimes.com/2018/09/29/opinion/sunday/christians-politics-belief.html.

———. "An Idol Is Anything That You Turn to and Say, 'Save Me.'" *Twitter,* January 22, 2022. https://twitter.com/timkellernyc/status/1484926361450029057.

———. "Roman Empire: 'You Christians Are Too Exclusive. You Threaten the Social Order Because You Won't Honor All Deities.' Modern West: 'You Christians Are Too Exclusive. You Threaten the Social Order Because You Won't Honor All Identities.'" *Twitter,* April 6, 2023. https://twitter.com/timkellernyc/status/1643922244060553223.

Kidd, Thomas. "Christian Discernment in Civic Engagement and Politics." *Baylor University,* January 19, 2021. https://www.baylor.edu/about/news.php?action=story&story=221591.

———. "The Coming Storm for Christian Higher Education." *The Gospel Coalition,* April 27, 2020. https://www.thegospelcoalition.org/blogs/evangelical-history/the-coming-storm-for-christian-higher-education/.

———. *Who Is an Evangelical? The History of a Movement in Crisis.* New Haven: Yale University Press, 2019.

Klein, Ezra. "Transcript: Ezra Klein Interviews Patrick Deneen." *The New York Times,* May 13, 2022. https://www.nytimes.com/2022/05/13/podcasts/transcript-ezra-klein-interviews-patrick-deneen.html.

Bibliography

Kristian, Bonnie. "2 Decades of Right Turns." *The Week*, December 30, 2021. https://theweek.com/articles/976288/2-decades-right-turns.

———. "Is There an Alternative to Christian Nationalism?" *Christianity Today*, June 30, 2022. https://www.christianitytoday.com/ct/2022/june-web-only/paul-miller-religion-american-greatness-nationalism.html.

———. *Untrustworthy: The Knowledge Crisis Breaking Our Brains, Polluting Our Politics, and Corrupting Christian Community*. Grand Rapids: Brazos, 2022.

Kruse, Kevin M. *One Nation Under God: How Corporate America Invented Christian America*. New York: Basic Books, 2015.

Kuga, Mitchell. "Some Libraries Are Facing Backlash Against LGBT Programs—And Holding Their Ground." *BuzzFeed*, November 15, 2018. https://www.buzzfeednews.com/article/mitchellkuga/librarians-drag-queen-story-hour-lgbt-safe-spaces.

Leeman, Jonathan. "Conservatives Clash on the Goal of Government." *Providence*, September 6, 2019. https://providencemag.com/2019/09/conservatives-clash-goal-government-sohrab-ahmari-david-french-debate/.

———. *How the Nations Rage: Rethinking Faith and Politics in a Divided Age*. Nashville: Thomas Nelson, 2018.

Leithart, Peter. "Against National Conservatism." *First Things*, August 19, 2022. https://www.firstthings.com/web-exclusives/2022/08/against-national-conservatism.

Lewis, Andrew R. *The Rights Turn in Conservative Christian Politics: How Abortion Transformed the Culture Wars*. New York: Cambridge University Press, 2017.

Lindsay, Michael. Personal interview, September 18, 2021.

Lowry, Rich. "Ron DeSantis and the New Republican Party." *National Review*, March 14, 2022. https://www.nationalreview.com/2022/03/ron-desantis-and-the-new-republican-party/.

Madison, James. "Federalist 10." *The Avalon Project: Documents in Law, History, and Diplomacy*, 1787. https://avalon.law.yale.edu/18th_century/fed10.asp.

Mangan, Dan. "Trump: I'll Appoint Supreme Court Justices to Overturn Roe v. Wade Abortion Case." *CNBC*, October 20, 2016. https://www.cnbc.com/2016/10/19/trump-ill-appoint-supreme-court-justices-to-overturn-roe-v-wade-abortion-case.html.

Marantz, Andrew. "Does Hungary Offer a Glimpse of Our Authoritarian Future?" *The New Yorker*, June 27, 2022. https://www.newyorker.com/magazine/2022/07/04/does-hungary-offer-a-glimpse-of-our-authoritarian-future.

Marcotte, Amanda. "Evangelicals Are Standing Up to Their Own Sexist Leaders." *Slate*, August 6, 2014. https://slate.com/human-interest/2014/08/protest-against-mark-driscoll-mars-hill-church-pastor-gets-called-out-by-his-flock.html.

Margolis, Michele F. *From Politics to the Pews: How Partisanship and the Political Environment Shape Religious Identity*. Chicago: University of Chicago Press, 2018.

Marquez, Alexandra. "The Rise of Theocracy among Conservatives." *NBC News*, September 15, 2022. https://www.nbcnews.com/meet-the-press/meetthepressblog/rise-theocracy-conservatives-meet-press-reports-rcna47586.

Marti, Gerardo. *American Blindspot: Race, Class, Religion, and the Trump Presidency*. Lanham, MD: Rowman & Littlefield, 2020.

Martínez, Jessica, and Gregory Smith. "How the Faithful Voted: A Preliminary 2016 Analysis." *Pew Research Center*, November 9, 2016. https://www.pewresearch.org/fact-tank/2016/11/09/how-the-faithful-voted-a-preliminary-2016-analysis/.

Bibliography

Mason, Lilliana. *Uncivil Agreement: How Politics Became Our Identity*. Chicago: University of Chicago Press, 2018.

Mason, Lilliana, and Julie Wronski. "One Tribe to Bind Them All: How Our Social Group Attachments Strengthen Partisanship." *Political Psychology* 39 (2018) 257–77.

McCarthy, Justin. "2017 Partisan Gap in Economic Confidence One of the Largest." *Gallup News*, February 2, 2018. https://news.gallup.com/poll/226649/2017-partisan-gap-economic-confidence-one-largest.aspx.

McCaulley, Esau. "The Racial Justice Debate Needs Civil Discourse, Not Straw Men." *Christianity Today*, August 10, 2021. https://www.christianitytoday.com/ct/2021/august-web-only/critical-race-theory-racial-justice-debate-civil-discourse.html.

McClellan, Hannah. "Christian Colleges Look for 'Missing Men.'" *Christianity Today*, August 25, 2022. https://www.christianitytoday.com/news/2022/august/missing-men-christian-college-male-recruitment.html.

———. "TIU Announces Plans to Move Undergrad Program Online." *Christianity Today*, February 20, 2023. https://www.christianitytoday.com/news/2023/february/tiu-trinity-university-undergrad-online-education-teds.html.

McDaniel, Eric. *Politics in the Pews: The Political Mobilization of Black Churches*. Ann Arbor: University of Michigan Press, 2008.

McLoud, Ian. "Why Our Neighborhoods Are Becoming More Partisan." *American Values Coalition*, February 23, 2022. https://americanvalues.org/blog/why-our-neighborhoods-are-becoming-more-partisan.

Meador, Jake. "The End of the Liberalism Debate." *Mere Orthodoxy*, November 16, 2021. https://mereorthodoxy.com/the-end-of-the-liberalism-debate/.

———. "One of the Persistent Problems Right Now in Evangelical Media and Publishing Is That We Have Historians and Sociologists Trying to Do Theological or Biblical Work and Unless You Are *extremely* Good, You Probably Can't Pull That Combo Off." *Twitter*, July 19, 2021. https://twitter.com/jake_meador/status/1417221280059772930.

Mendoza, Jessica. "How a California Bill Became a Lesson in Compromise." *Christian Science Monitor*, August 12, 2016. https://www.csmonitor.com/USA/Society/2016/0812/How-a-California-bill-became-a-lesson-in-compromise.

Merritt, Jonathan. "I Believe David Platt Is a Well-Meaning Pastor and Not Some Power-Hungry Celebrity Leader. AND I Also Believe He Made a Bad Decision That Confused and Caused Pain among Many Minorities and Marginalized Christians. One Can Assert the Later and Still Hold the Former." *Twitter*, June 4, 2019. https://twitter.com/JonathanMerritt/status/1135996415983915009.

Metaxas, Eric. "'For Nothing Is Secret That Will Not Be Revealed, nor Anything Hidden That Will Not Be Known and Come to Light.' — #Jesus." *Twitter*, December 6, 2020. https://twitter.com/ericmetaxas/status/1335584712673390592.

———. "If the American People Actually Had Elected Joe Biden to the Presidency, This Would Trouble Me More." *Twitter*, April 21, 2021. https://twitter.com/ericmetaxas/status/1384740522749661184.

———. "Who Is Running the Country??? We Know It Cannot Be Joe Biden, Because We Watch His 'Appearances' and See He Is a Doddering Husk of His Former Self. So Who IS Running the Nation? This Is THE Developing Scandal of Our Time. Just Watch. Https://T.Co/MnlwhZJj48." *Twitter*, March 10, 2021. https://twitter.com/ericmetaxas/status/1369669109391179778.

Bibliography

Miller, Emily. "Neighborly Faith Urges Evangelicals to Find a 'third Way' to Befriend Muslims." *Religion News Service*, November 6, 2019. https://religionnews.com/2019/11/06/neighborly-faith-urges-evangelicals-to-find-a-third-way-to-befriend-muslims/.

Miller, Eric. "The Market Made Me Do It: The Scandal of the Evangelical College." *Mere Orthodoxy*, September 23, 2020. https://mereorthodoxy.com/market-made-scandal-evangelical-college/.

Miller, Paul. D. "Against 'Conservative Democracy.'" *Providence*, June 19, 2019. https://providencemag.com/2019/06/against-conservative-democracy/.

———. *The Religion of American Greatness: What's Wrong with Christian Nationalism.* Downers Grove, IL: IVP Academic, 2022.

Montague, Zach. "Holding It Aloft, He Incited a Backlash. What Does the Bible Mean to Trump?" *The New York Times*, June 3, 2020. https://www.nytimes.com/2020/06/02/us/politics/trump-bible-st-johns.html.

Moore, Russell, and Luke Goodrich. "How Eagle Feathers and Copper Mines Might Alter Your Religious Liberty." *Christianity Today*, November 23, 2021. https://christianitytoday.com/ct/2021/november-web-only/religious-freedom-restoration-act-copper-mines.html.

Morris, Shane. "Politics and Prophetic Witness: Samuel James On Criticizing Both Political Tribes (Episode 49)." *Upstream*, June 15, 2021. https://upstreamcc.libsyn.com/politics-and-prophetic-witness-samuel-james-on-criticizing-both-political-tribes-episode-49.

Mui, Ylan, Jacob Pramuk, and Mallika Mitra. "White House, Congress Strike a Two-Year Debt Ceiling and Budget Deal." *CNBC*, July 22, 2019. https://www.cnbc.com/2019/07/22/us-debt-ceiling-and-budget-deal-near-final-suspends-ceiling-for-2-years-source.html.

Noble, Alan. "Christian Colleges Are in Crisis. Here's What That Means for the Church." *Christianity Today*, September 10, 2020. https://www.christianitytoday.com/ct/2020/september-web-only/alan-noble-christian-college-crisis-cccu-church.html.

———. *You Are Not Your Own: Belonging to God in an Inhuman World.* Downers Grove, IL: InterVarsity, 2021.

Obergefell v. Hodges, 576 U.S. 644 (2015).

Onishi, Bradley. "Is Abortion No Longer Significant for Evangelicals—or Has It Just Become Like Water?" *Religion Dispatches*, August 12, 2021. https://religiondispatches.org/is-abortion-no-longer-significant-for-evangelicals-or-has-it-just-become-like-water/.

Ortlund, Gavin. "Evangelical Self-Criticism: A Plea for Openness." *GavinOrtlund.com*, February 26, 2022. https://gavinortlund.com/2022/02/26/evangelical-self-criticism-a-plea-for-openness/.

Parks, Kristine. "Media Meltdown over Supreme Court Ruling in Favor of Religious Schools: 'Prime Christian Nationalist Stuff.'" Fox News, June 22, 2022. https://www.foxnews.com/media/media-meltdown-supreme-court-ruling-favor-religious-schools-christian-nationalist-stuff.

Perkins, Tony. "Why Christians Must Support Religious Freedom for Everyone." *Religion News Service*, June 19, 2019. https://religionnews.com/2019/06/19/why-christians-must-support-religious-freedom-for-everyone/.

Perry, Samuel L., and Andrew L. Whitehead. "Christian Nationalism and White Racial Boundaries: Examining Whites' Opposition to Interracial Marriage." *Ethnic and Racial Studies* 38 (2015) 1671–89.

Bibliography

Perry, Samuel L., Andrew L. Whitehead, and Joshua B. Grubbs. "Culture Wars and COVID-19 Conduct: Christian Nationalism, Religiosity, and Americans' Behavior during the Coronavirus Pandemic." *Journal for the Scientific Study of Religion* 59 (2020) 405–16.

Pew Research Center. "Faith on the Hill." January 4, 2021. https://www.pewresearch.org/religion/2021/01/04/faith-on-the-hill-2021/.

———. "In U.S., Decline of Christianity Continues at Rapid Pace." October 17, 2019. https://www.pewforum.org/2019/10/17/in-u-s-decline-of-christianity-continues-at-rapid-pace/.

———. "Majority of Public Disapproves of Supreme Court's Decision To Overturn Roe v. Wade." July 6, 2022. https://www.pewresearch.org/politics/2022/07/06/majority-of-public-disapproves-of-supreme-courts-decision-to-overturn-roe-v-wade/.

———. "Religious Landscape Study." https://www.pewresearch.org/religion/religious-landscape-study/.

Pierce, Matthew. *Evangelical Thought Leader: The Liturgy of Radically Engaging the Culture of Paradigm Shifts.* Independently published, 2021.

Pierson, Patrick. "Dogmatic Partisanship's Dead End." *Mere Orthodoxy*, October 30, 2020. https://mereorthodoxy.com/dogmatic-partisanships-dead-end/.

Planned Parenthood of Southeastern Pennsylvania v. Casey, 505 U.S. 833 (1992).

Plessy v. Ferguson, 163 U.S. 537 (1896).

Pollard, Chip. Personal interview, September 22, 2021.

Public Religion Research Institute. "The 2020 Census of American Religion." July 8, 2021. https://www.prri.org/research/2020-census-of-american-religion/.

Putnam, Robert D. *Bowling Alone: The Collapse and Revival of American Community.* London: Touchstone, 2001.

Radney, Derek. "Here Is Where James & Rennites Miss Keller. Being Winsome & Engaging Others with Charity Was Not a Strategy but a Conviction Abt How Christians Should Always Treat Others, Even If It Fails to Gain a Hearing." *Twitter*, May 6, 2022. https://twitter.com/derekradney/status/1522685893030592518.

Redden, Elizabeth. "Religious Freedom vs. Freedom From Discrimination." *Inside Higher Ed*, April 6, 2021. https://www.insidehighered.com/news/2021/04/06/lgbt-students-sue-education-department-over-title-ix-religious-exemption.

Reformed Church in America. "The Heidelberg Catechism." https://www.rca.org/about/theology/creeds-and-confessions/the-heidelberg-catechism/.

Relevant. "Poll: Evangelical Pastors Divided on Whether Racism or CRT Is a Bigger Threat to the Church," *Relevant*, February 16, 2022. https://relevantmagazine.com/faith/church/poll-evangelical-pastors-think-crt-is-as-big-a-threat-to-the-american-church-as-racism/.

Renn, Aaron. "The Three Worlds of Evangelicalism." *First Things*, February 1, 2022. https://www.firstthings.com/article/2022/02/the-three-worlds-of-evangelicalism.

Rienzi, Mark. "Symposium: Amid Polarization and Chaos, the Court Charts a Path toward Peaceful Pluralism." *SCOTUSblog*, August 5, 2020. https://www.scotusblog.com/2020/08/symposium-amid-polarization-and-chaos-the-court-charts-a-path-toward-peaceful-pluralism/.

Riley, Claudette. "If You Kneel, the Game Is over, C of O Tells Opposing Teams." *Springfield News-Leader*, September 29, 2017. https://www.news-leader.com/story/news/education/2017/09/29/no-pledge-no-play-policy-college-ozarks-student-athletes/717937001/.

Bibliography

Roach, David. "How Southern Baptists Became Pro-Life." *Baptist Press*, January 16, 2015. https://www.baptistpress.com/resource-library/news/how-southern-baptists-became-pro-life/.

Robertson, Abigail. "Pro-Life Evangelicals for Biden Feel Betrayed COVID Relief Bill Excludes Hyde." *CBN News*, March 8, 2021. https://www1.cbn.com/cbnnews/politics/2021/march/pro-life-evangelicals-for-biden-feel-betrayed-covid-relief-bill-excludes-hyde.

Roe v. Wade, 410 U.S. 113 (1973).

Ross, Janell. "Who, Exactly, Is David French, the 'Never Trump' White Knight Candidate?" *The Washington Post*, June 1, 2016. https://www.washingtonpost.com/news/the-fix/wp/2016/06/01/who-exactly-is-david-french-the-never-trump-white-knight-candidate/.

Sayet, Evan. "He May Be Crass, but This Man Fights." *The Providence Journal*, July 25, 2017. https://www.providencejournal.com/story/opinion/2017/07/25/my-turn-evan-sayet-trump-may-be-crass-but-he-fights/8339571007/.

Schaeffer, Francis A. *A Christian Manifesto*. Wheaton, IL: Crossway, 1981.

———. *The Great Evangelical Disaster*. Wheaton, IL: Crossway, 1984.

Schreiner, Patrick. *Political Gospel: Public Witness in a Politically Crazy World*. Nashville: B&H, 2022.

Seidel, Andrew L. *American Crusade: How the Supreme Court Is Weaponizing Religious Freedom*. New York: Union Square & Co., 2022.

———. *The Founding Myth: Why Christian Nationalism Is Un-American*. New York: Union Square & Co., 2019.

Sheiner, Wendy Edelberg, and Louise Sheiner. "How Worried Should We Be If the Debt Ceiling Isn't Lifted?" *Brookings Institution*, September 28, 2021. https://www.brookings.edu/blog/up-front/2021/09/28/how-worried-should-we-be-if-the-debt-ceiling-isnt-lifted/.

Siegel, Ethan. "Newt Gingrich Exemplifies Just How Unscientific America Is." *Forbes*, August 5, 2016. https://www.forbes.com/sites/startswithabang/2016/08/05/newt-gingrich-exemplifies-just-how-unscientific-america-is/.

Silliman, Daniel. "Knock Knock. It's Weird Evangelical Twitter." *Christianity Today*, April 20, 2020. https://www.christianitytoday.com/ct/2020/may-june/weird-evangelical-twitter.html.

Slade, Stephanie. "The New Theocrats Are Neither Conservative Nor Christian." *Reason*, June 3, 2019. https://reason.com/2019/06/03/the-new-theocrats-are-neither-conservative-nor-christian/.

Slisco, Aila. "Ted Cruz Tells Students His Pronoun Is 'Kiss My A**' in Gender Identity Jab." *Newsweek*, July 22, 2022. https://www.newsweek.com/ted-cruz-tells-students-his-pronoun-kiss-my-gender-identity-jab-1727340.

Smethurst, Matt. "If You're Outraged at Everything, You're Not like Jesus. (Matt. 12:20) If You're Outraged at Nothing, You're Not like Jesus. (Matt. 21:12)." *Twitter*, July 15, 2015. https://twitter.com/MattSmethurst/status/621118488812216320.

Smietana, Bob. "How Eric Metaxas Went from Trump Despiser to True Believer." *Religion News Service*, December 3, 2020. https://religionnews.com/2020/12/03/metaxas-jesus-trump-stolen-election-christian-nationalism-rod-dreher-sidney-powell/.

Smith, Christian, and Melina Lundquist Denton. *Soul Searching: The Religious and Spiritual Lives of American Teenagers*. Oxford: Oxford University Press, 2009.

BIBLIOGRAPHY

Smith, Gregory. "About Three-in-Ten U.S. Adults Are Now Religiously Unaffiliated." Pew Research Center, December 14, 2021. https://www.pewresearch.org/religion/2021/12/14/about-three-in-ten-u-s-adults-are-now-religiously-unaffiliated/.

———. "More White Americans Adopted than Shed Evangelical Label during Trump Presidency, Especially His Supporters." Pew Research Center, September 15, 2021. https://www.pewresearch.org/fact-tank/2021/09/15/more-white-americans-adopted-than-shed-evangelical-label-during-trump-presidency-especially-his-supporters/.

Smith, Matthew. "Christian Universities Need a Reset." *The Gospel Coalition*, February 28, 2022. https://www.thegospelcoalition.org/article/christian-universities-reset/.

Stackaruk, Chris, and Kevin Singer. "Who Is Influencing Young Evangelicals on Politics?" *Neighborly Faith*, November 2022. https://www.neighborlyfaith.org/evangelicals-politics-report.

Steinmetz, Katy. "See Obama's 20-Year Evolution on LGBT Rights." *Time*, April 10, 2015. https://time.com/3816952/obama-gay-lesbian-transgender-lgbt-rights/.

Stern, Mark Joseph. "Neil Gorsuch Just Handed Down a Historic Victory for LGBTQ Rights." *Slate*, June 15, 2020. https://slate.com/news-and-politics/2020/06/supreme-court-lgbtq-discrimination-employment.html.

Strode, Tom. "ERLC's Moore Defends Religious Freedom for Muslims." *Baptist Press*, June 16, 2016. https://www.baptistpress.com/resource-library/news/erlcs-moore-defends-religious-freedom-for-muslims/.

Sullivan, Becky. "The Proportion of White Christians In The U.S. Has Stopped Shrinking, New Study Finds." *NPR*, July 8, 2021. https://www.npr.org/2021/07/08/1014047885/americas-white-christian-plurality-has-stopped-shrinking-a-new-study-finds.

Thrush, Glenn. "Basking in Olympic Snub Risky for GOP." *NBC 6 South Florida*, October 5, 2009. https://www.nbcmiami.com/news/politics/basking_in_olympic_snub_risky_for_gop/2052071/.

Tisby, Jemar. *The Color of Compromise: The Truth about the American Church's Complicity in Racism*. Grand Rapids: Zondervan, 2019.

Tocqueville, Alexis de. *Democracy in America*. Chicago: University of Chicago Press, 2002.

"Toward a More Responsible Two-Party System: A Report of the Committee on Political Parties, American Political Science Association." *American Political Science Review* 44 (1950) 1–96.

Trueman, Carl R. *The Rise and Triumph of the Modern Self: Cultural Amnesia, Expressive Individualism, and the Road to Sexual Revolution*. Wheaton, IL: Crossway, 2020.

U.S. v. Windsor, 570 U.S. 744 (2013).

Vallier, Kevin. "Why Are Americans So Distrustful of Each Other?" *The Wall Street Journal*, December 17, 2020. https://www.wsj.com/articles/why-are-americans-so-distrustful-of-each-other-11608217988.

VanderWeele, Tyler J., and Brendan Case. "Empty Pews Are an American Public Health Crisis." *Christianity Today*, October 19, 2021. https://www.christianitytoday.com/ct/2021/november/church-empty-pews-are-american-public-health-crisis.html.

Walker, Andrew. "Bostock Is as Bad as You Think." *Christianity Today*, June 19, 2020. https://www.christianitytoday.com/ct/2020/june-web-only/bostock-is-as-bad-as-you-think.html.

———. *Liberty for All: Defending Everyone's Religious Freedom in a Pluralistic Age*. Grand Rapids: Brazos, 2021.

Bibliography

———. "The Rule of Roe Is over and Its Scourge of Violence and Injustice No More. One of the Most Important Days in American History." *Twitter*, June 24, 2022. https://twitter.com/andrewtwalk/status/1540337703706927104.

———. "What Does 'Christian Nationalism' Even Mean?" *World*, October 25, 2022. https://wng.org/opinions/what-does-christian-nationalism-even-mean-1666700202.

Wallace-Wells, Benjamin. "David French, Sohrab Ahmari, and the Battle for the Future of Conservatism." *The New Yorker*, September 12, 2019. https://www.newyorker.com/news/the-political-scene/david-french-sohrab-ahmari-and-the-battle-for-the-future-of-conservatism.

———. "How a Conservative Activist Invented the Conflict Over Critical Race Theory." *The New Yorker*, June 18, 2021. https://www.newyorker.com/news/annals-of-inquiry/how-a-conservative-activist-invented-the-conflict-over-critical-race-theory.

———. "What American Conservatives See in Hungary's Leader." *The New Yorker*, September 13, 2021. https://www.newyorker.com/news/annals-of-inquiry/what-rod-dreher-sees-in-viktor-orban.

Wear, Michael. "As Someone Who Worked Very Hard to Try to Set a Standard for Responsible, Ethical Religious Engagement from The White House, It Is Heartbreaking and Infuriating to See a POTUS Who Has Fallen Short of Every Standard and Broken Every Sense of Propriety and Respect and Humility." *Twitter*, June 1, 2020. https://twitter.com/MichaelRWear/status/1267598679621451776.

———. "Power and Sacrifice." *Reclaiming Hope Newsletter*, December 22, 2021. https://reclaiminghope.substack.com/p/power-and-sacrifice.

———. "Presidents Visit Churches—but Not the Way Trump Did." *The Washington Post*, June 5, 2019. https://www.washingtonpost.com/religion/2019/06/05/presidents-visit-churches-not-like-trump-did/.

Webster, Steven W. "Anger and Social Polarization Are Bipartisan Phenomena. Https://Journals.Uchicago.Edu/Doi/10.1086/718979." *Twitter*, February 24, 2022. https://twitter.com/stevenwwebster/status/1496838577514287115.

Webster, Steven W., Adam N. Glynn, and Matthew P. Motta. "Partisan Schadenfreude and Candidate Cruelty." May 11, 2022. http://stevenwwebster.com/research/schadenfreude.pdf.

Weigel, David, Colby Itkowitz, and Arjun Singh. "GOP's Meijer Voted to Impeach Trump. Now Democrats Are Targeting Him." *The Washington Post*, July 27, 2022. https://www.washingtonpost.com/politics/2022/07/27/meijer-trump-impeachment-democrats/.

Wester, Joshua. "Why Would Christians Support Religious Freedom?" *ERLC*, November 2, 2020. https://erlc.com/resource-library/articles/why-would-christians-support-religious-freedom/.

Whitehead, Andrew L., and Samuel L. Perry. "A More Perfect Union? Christian Nationalism and Support for Same-Sex Unions." *Sociological Perspectives* 58 (2015) 422–40.

———. *Taking America Back for God: Christian Nationalism in the United States*. New York: Oxford University Press, 2020.

Whitehead, Andrew L., Samuel L. Perry, and Joseph O. Baker. "Make America Christian Again: Christian Nationalism and Voting for Donald Trump in the 2016 Presidential Election." *Sociology of Religion* 79 (2018) 147–71.

Whitehead, Andrew L., Landon Schnabel, and Samuel L. Perry. "Gun Control in the Crosshairs: Christian Nationalism and Opposition to Stricter Gun Laws." *Socius* 4 (2018) 1–13.

Bibliography

Whitehead, John. "Fact-Checking Randall Balmer's Urban Legend on the Real Origin of the Religious Right." *The Gospel Coalition*, August 2, 2022. https://www.thegospelcoalition.org/blogs/evangelical-history/fact-checking-randall-balmers-urban-legend-on-the-real-origin-of-the-religious-right/.

Wilken, Robert Louis. *Liberty in the Things of God: The Christian Origins of Religious Freedom*. New Haven: Yale University Press, 2019.

Wilkinson, Alissa. "Everybody Worships." *Books and Culture*, June 2015. https://www.booksandculture.com/articles/2015/mayjun/everybody-worships.html.

Wilson, Andrew. "It's Hamilton's World. We're Just Living in It." *Christianity Today*, February 14, 2022. https://www.christianitytoday.com/ct/2022/march/hamilton-parable-post-christian-west-andrew-wilson.html.

Wolfe, Stephen. *The Case for Christian Nationalism*. Moscow, ID: Canon, 2022.

Wolfe, William. "Christians Actually Are Being Persecuted in America." *Twitter*, July 11, 2022. https://twitter.com/William_E_Wolfe/status/1546520384270471169.

———. "Cracker Barrel Christians vs. Elite Evangelicals." *Standing for Freedom Center*, October 29, 2021. https://www.standingforfreedom.com/2021/10/cracker-barrel-christians-vs-elite-evangelicals/.

———. "Here's One of the Biggest Problems with Conservatives in America: They Would Rather Lose Nobly, Even to Wicked & Evil Enemies, than Win in an Ugly Manner. They Want to Feel Good about Themselves, Though They Let Their Country Be Overrun by Tyrants, Then Do What It Takes to Win." *Twitter*, October 26, 2022. https://twitter.com/william_e_wolfe/status/1585010003542700032?s=46&t=s5eCkD3X12mNtBsHezc8ow.

———. "It's a Pitched Battle Right Now, Not Some Quiet, Peaceful Pasture Where the Secularists Have Their Corner and We Have Ours. They Are Coming for Us at Every Turn—Schools, Commerce, in the Public Square—and They Will Use Every Means of Power They Can to Silence Us or Lock Us Up." *Twitter*, July 11, 2022. https://twitter.com/William_E_Wolfe/status/1546524240417099777.

Wood, James R. "How I Evolved on Tim Keller." *First Things*, May 6, 2022. https://www.firstthings.com/web-exclusives/2022/05/how-i-evolved-on-tim-keller.

———. "The Limits of Winsome Politics." *The American Conservative*, September 21, 2022. https://www.theamericanconservative.com/the-limits-of-winsome-politics/.

———. "This Article Is Not About Tim Keller." *American Reformer*, May 12, 2022. https://americanreformer.com/2022/05/this-article-is-not-about-tim-keller/.

Wood, Peter. "Academia Needs Builders, Not Burners: What Charlie Kirk Gets Wrong About Higher Education." *Minding the Campus*, August 2, 2022. https://www.mindingthecampus.org/2022/08/02/academia-needs-builders-not-burners-what-charlie-kirk-gets-wrong-about-higher-education/.

Wood, Tom. "Elite and Mass Polarization, 1970–2020. Data from @electionstudies and DWNOMINATE. Https://T.Co/XdueT5hby8." *Twitter*, February 22, 2022. https://twitter.com/thomasjwood/status/1496141830701920269.

Yancey, George. "Is There Really Anti-Christian Discrimination in America?" *The Gospel Coalition*, August 19, 2019. https://www.thegospelcoalition.org/article/anti-christian-discrimination-america/.

Zerofsky, Elisabeth. "How the American Right Fell in Love With Hungary." *The New York Times*, October 19, 2021. https://www.nytimes.com/2021/10/19/magazine/viktor-orban-rod-dreher.html.

Index

2020 election, xiii, 9, 28, 31, 93
abortion, 44–45, 49, 59
    and Biden presidency, xiv-xv
    and evangelical politics, 4–8, 13–14, 17, 65
    and Trump Supreme Court nominations, 72
    and vote choice, 118–119, 121–124
    as culture war issue, 24–25, 31–32
    as moral problem, 66
Abramowitz, Alan, 29
Ahmari, Sohrab, 80, 83–84
American Enterprise Institute, 27, 39
American Family Association, 7
American National Election Study, 24
American Political Science Association, 19–20
American Values Coalition, 27
Anderson, Matthew Lee, 104
Asbury University, 106
Augustine, 2

Balmer, Randall, 13–14
Barton, David, 34–35
Basham, Megan, 111
Baucham, Voddie, 16
Biden, Joe, xiii, 53, 62, 112
    and American Rescue Plan, xiv
    and abortion, xiv-xv, 7, 119
    evangelical disappointment in, xiv-xv
Bilbro, Jeff, 27, 77
Bird, Michael, 114
Bishop, Bill, 27
Black Protestants, 15, 38, 53, 118
Blake, Nathaniel, 83

Bob Jones University, 13–14
Bonhoeffer, Dietrich, xiii
Bostock v. Clayton County, 79–81, 86
Brody, David, 2
Brooks, David, 77
Brown, Kevin, 106–107
Burge, Ryan, 40, 98, 104

Calvin, John, 2
Carney, Timothy, 41
Carroll, Dave, 101
Carter, Jimmy, 6, 10–11, 29
Christian Coalition, 7
Christian nationalism, 36, 89–91, 92
Churchill, Winston, 79
civil religion, 50, 62, 77
Civil Rights Act, 80
civil rights movement, 1, 13, 15, 17, 126
civil war, 20, 125–126, 127
Clinton, Bill, 7, 32, 118
common good originalism, 81
Concerned Women for America, 7
Congressional Freethought Caucus, 90
Converse, Phillip, 21–25
Cooper, Anderson, 27
Council for Christian Colleges and Universities, 103, 108
Covenant College, 107
COVID-19 pandemic, xiv, 1, 28, 104
Cox, Daniel, 39–40, 104
Critical race theory, 12–13, 16
Cruz, Ted, 12, 24, 76

Darling, Dan, 113
debt ceiling, 56–57

Index

Declaration of Independence, 84
Deneen, Patrick, 75–76, 78, 81–82, 83, 106
Denton, Melinda Lundquist, 99
DeSantis, Ron, 11
DeYoung, Kevin, 90–91
Djupe, Paul, 42
Dobbs v. Jackson Women's Health, 8, 31
drag queen story hour, 79–81
Dreher, Rod, 69, 76, 82, 96
Dred Scott v. Sandford, 17
Driscoll, Mark, 9
Durkheim, Emile, 48
Duverger's law, 20

Eagle Forum, 7
Edsall, Thomas, 25–26
Eldredge, John, 8
Emerson, Michael, 13
Enneagram, 52
Equal Rights Amendment, 7
Ewing, Patrick, 56
expressive individualism, 45–48, 77, 83, 97, 99

Falwell, Jerry, 6
Family Research Council, 7, 87
Fea, John, 16
Fiorina, Morris, 24–25
First Amendment, 8, 13, 34, 38, 79
Flowers, Skyler, 110
Floyd, George, 1
Fox News, 16, 90
Franklin, Benjamin, 34
French, David, 75, 111
    and drag queen story hour, 79–80
    as "Never Trump" figure, 59–60
    on liberalism, 84–85
    on post-Christian politics, 68
    responding to Aaron Renn, 63–64
Freud, Sigmund, 45

Gallup, 48
Geneva College, 105
George Fox University, 102–103
Gerson, Michael, 2
Giboney, Justin, 59–60, 120

Goodrich, Luke, 88
Gorsuch, Neil, 80–81
Gospel Coalition, xii, 68, 98, 104
    and evangelical Christian witness, 115
    and political discipleship, 101
Graham, Billy, 10
Graham, Franklin, xi
Graham, Michael, 110
Great Depression, The, 126
Greene, Marjorie Taylor, 112
Greenhut, Steven, 79–80

Hall, Mark David, 35, 89–90
Hammer, Josh, 77, 81
Hansen, Colin, 98, 104
Hatfield, Mark, 24
Hawkins, Matthew, 101
Heidelberg Catechism, 45, 47
Hochman, Nate, 49
Hoogstra, Shirley, 95, 103
Huckabee, Tyler, 71
Hutchinson, Asa, 120
Hyde Amendment, xiv-xv, 7

Inazu, John, 84
Internal Revenue Service, 13
Iran-Contra scandal, 10

James, Samuel, 70, 72, 115
January 6, 31, 59
Jefferson, Thomas, 20, 34
Jewish exile, 70
John Birch Society, 7
John Brown University, 52, 95, 103, 105, 108
Jones, Robert, 14–15

Kaemingk, Matthew, 88
Kalmoe, Nathan, 30–31
Kavanaugh, Brett, 19
Keller, Tim, 52
    and political engagement, 68, 111
    and "third way" politics, 71
    James Wood's critique of, 63
    on idolizing politics, 74, 128
Kidd, Thomas, 6, 103
King, Martin Luther, Jr., 110

Index

King's College, The, 104
Klein, Ezra, 106
Kobes du Mez, Kristin, 9–11
Kristian, Bonnie, 32, 67, 90
Kruse, Kevin, 16
Kuyper, Abraham, xv, 103

Leeman, Jonathan, 66, 84
Leithart, Peter, 92
Lewis, Andrew, 7–8
Lifeway Research, 16
Lincoln, Abraham, xiv
Lindsay, Michael, 105
The Lion, the Witch, and the Wardrobe, 112
Locke, John, 78
Luther, Martin, xiii, 2

Madison, James, 32, 68, 85
Margolis, Michele, 42
Mars Hill Church, 9
Marti, Gerardo, 16
Marx, Karl, 45
Mason, Liliana, 25–28, 30–31, 50
McClean Bible Church, xi
Meador, Jake, 93
Meijer, Peter, 58–60
Merritt, Jonathan, xii
Metaxas, Eric, xiii–xv, xviii
Miller, Paul, 89, 92
Miranda, Lin Manuel, 126
Moore, Russell, 68, 87, 111
Moral Majority, 6–7
moralistic therapeutic deism, 97, 99

National Conservatism Conference, 76–77, 91–92
negative partisanship, 28–31, 33, 127
    as threat to Christian politics, 56
    temptation of, 69, 71, 108
Neighborly Faith, 88, 100
Neiheisel, Jacob, 42
New Deal, 15–16
Nietzsche, Friedrich, 45
Nixon, Richard, 10, 15
Noble, Alan, 47–48, 109
North, Oliver, 10–11

Obama, Barack, xiii, 2
    and 2016 Olympics, 30
    and abortion, 59
    and same-sex marriage, 118
    and the debt ceiling, 57
Obergefell v. Hodges, 47, 62, 64
O'Connor, Sandra Day, 6
Onishi, Bradley, 7
Orban, Viktor, 69, 76, 82, 91
Ortlund, Gavin, 111

Perkins, Tony, 87
Pew Research Center, 8, 38–39, 42
Pierce, Matthew, 73
Pierson, Patrick, 32
Platt, David, xi–xii, xv, xviii
Pro-Life Evangelicals for Biden, xiv
Planned Parenthood v. Casey, 5
Plessy v. Ferguson, 17
Pollard, Chip, 105
Putnam, Robert, 40, 48
Public Religion Research Institute, 38–39

Radney, Derek, 63
Reagan, Ronald, 6–7, 10, 15, 29, 32
Reed, Ralph, 2
religious freedom, 108, 119
    and Christian nationalism, 90
    and LGBTQ rights, 81
    and pluralism, 86–88
    and Trump Supreme Court nominations, 72
    as culture war issue, 32, 49
Religious Freedom Restoration Act, 32
Renn, Aaron, 43–44, 62, 64, 67, 100
Respect for Marriage Act, 86
Rienzi, Mark, 86
Roe v. Wade, 5–8, 17, 65
Rufo, Christopher, 12

Sagal, Peter, 27
Schaeffer, Francis, 5–6, 14, 44–45
schadenfreude, 27, 29–31, 33
Schreiner, Patrick, 101, 115
September 11, 50
Singer, Kevin, 88
Slade, Stephanie, 92

Index

Smietana, Bob, xiv
Smith, Christian, 13, 99
Smethurst, Matt, 68
social polarization, 26–28, 32–33, 37, 50, 108
Southern Baptist Convention, 6
Spicer, Sean, 56
St. John's Episcopal Church, 1
Stupak, Bart, 58–60

Taylor, Breonna, 1
Tertullian, 87
"Three Worlds of Evangelicalism," 43–44, 62, 100
Tisby, Jemar, 15
Trinity International University, 104
Trueman, Carl, 45–47, 97
Trump, Donald, 16
    and 2016 election, 56
    and 2020 election, xiii-xiv, 28
    and abortion, 6–7
    and Bible incident, 1–2
    and political violence, 31
    as fighter, 11
    Christian support for, 49
    prayer for, xi-xii

United States v. Windsor, 47

Vallier, Kevin, 28

Wear, Michael, xiii, 2–3, 85
Walker, Andrew, 8, 51, 87, 91
Wallace, David Foster, 122
Webster, Steven, 28–30
Wenger, Ted, 70, 99
Wester, Joshua, 87
White House Office on Faith-Based and Neighborhood Partnerships, 2
Whitehead, Jon, 14
Wilson, Andrew, 127
Wolfe, Stephen, 83, 89–90
Wolfe, William, 34–36, 69, 110
Wood, James, 63–66
Wood, Peter, 106

www.ingramcontent.com/pod-product-compliance
Lightning Source LLC
Chambersburg PA
CBHW022120160426
43197CB00009B/1096